SPECIAL
SERMONS
FOR SPECIAL DAYS

SPECIAL
SERMONS
FOR SPECIAL DAYS

*Eighteen Condensed Sermons
for the
Twentieth Century*

By

GEORGE SWEETING

MOODY PRESS
CHICAGO

Library of Congress Cataloging in Publication Data

Sweeting, George, 1924-
  Special sermons for special days.

  1. Occasional sermons. 2. Sermons, American. I. Title.

BV4254.2.S93   252   77-1218

ISBN 0-8024-8206-6

*Dedicated
to that very select company
of pastors who attend
the flock of God.*

With warm appreciation to Wayne Christianson, Mark Sweeney, and Judy Paney, who have assisted me in research and script writing.

CONTENTS

ONE

THE NEW YEAR AND FEAR

INTRODUCTION

Stepping through the door into a new year should be an exciting experience. Yet for millions of people, the adventure of entering the New Year is overshadowed by fear.

The cold breath of fear knows all ages and every walk of life. Some people are afraid to go to the supermarket or corner store even in broad daylight. Others are afraid they may not find a job. Parents are afraid that the next ring of the phone might bring bad news about their children. Sick people are afraid of what the doctor may say the next time they go to see him. And thousands are afraid of the future. Fear, without a doubt, is one of the great enemies of successful living.

Not long ago, a group of distinguished scholars met in Chicago. They listened as a noted scientist gave a very gloomy picture of the next twenty-five years. He reported that a person born today may well live to be a hundred years old. During that time, he will possibly see the world run out of oil and natural gas. He may also see a massive drought across America, worldwide famine, and a major American city leveled by an earthquake. That's a very dark and gloomy forecast.

Despite the many reports like this, the future does have great possibilities. There are many exciting prospects for the years ahead. Yet fear itself is destructive. Like a drop of ink in a glass of water, a little is enough to color everything.

Fear does not depend on how good or bad conditions are. It depends on our response to them. Fear can tie us in knots. It can paralyze our thinking and our actions. It can make our lives a living hell.

What is fear? The dictionary defines it as a "painful emotion marked by alarm or dread or disquiet." It is response to what we think may be unpleasant.

Fear is as old as sin. It began in the Garden of Eden the day that Adam and Eve disobeyed God. In Genesis 3:8, we find Adam and Eve hiding fearfully from God "amongst the trees of the garden."

Ever since that tragic day, fear has followed every member of the human race. We fear as babies. We have fears in our childhood and great and growing fears in our youth. More fears hound us through adulthood and even in old age.

But then, not all fear is bad. The fear that keeps a small child from stepping into a busy street may save his life. As adults, we need the kind of fear that keeps us from touching a high-voltage wire or driving through a stoplight. Yes, there are some fears that are helpful.

Above all else, we need the fear of God: a reverential respect and awe for the God who made us. Repeatedly the Bible tells us that it is the fear of the Lord which is the beginning of wisdom.

Do you have this kind of fear—a reverential respect and awe for God? Only those who do can expect to know Him and enjoy His blessings.

Three times in Psalm 103—that wonderful poem of thankfulness—David reminds us that God's blessings are only for "them that fear him." This kind of fear is the kind that blesses, that builds, that strengthens.

The kind of fear that burdens is something else. It is an anxious fear, a fear that chills and freezes and kills. God is against this fear. Again and again, when God has spoken to men, His first words have been, "Fear not." Don't be afraid.

The key to overcoming fear is faith: faith in God. He loves us, and He holds the future. If we fear the future, we do not have faith. If we have faith, we cannot live in fear.

The Bible says that anxious fear is sin. In fact, Revelation 21

10

puts fear first in a list of sins that will keep men out of heaven. Notice how verse 8 begins: "But the fearful, and unbelieving, and the abominable, and murderers, and whoremongers, and sorcerers, and idolaters, and all liars, shall have their part in . . . the second death." You see, God wants us to walk in faith, not fear.

For years, God's servant David was hounded by King Saul. But he found help. "I sought the LORD," he writes in Psalm 34: 4, "and he heard me, and delivered me from all my fears." David looked to the Lord and found relief. In the same psalm, he adds, "The angel of the LORD encampeth round about them that fear him, and delivereth them" (v. 7).

My friend, this is the promise of God in His Word.

Put God first in your life. Respect and reverence Him, and He will deliver you from fear. Consider some of the promises of Scripture:

Psalm 23:4, "Yea, though I walk through the valley of the shadow of death, I will fear no evil."

Psalm 27:1, "The LORD is my light and my salvation: whom shall I fear? the LORD is the strength of my life; of whom shall I be afraid?"

Psalm 32:7, "Thou art my hiding place; thou shalt preserve me from trouble; thou shalt compass me about with songs of deliverance."

Psalm 34:9, "O fear the LORD, ye his saints: for there is no want to them that fear him."

Psalm 56:3, "What time I am afraid, I will trust in thee."

Psalm 91:2, "I will say of the LORD, He is my refuge and my fortress: my God; in him will I trust."

Psalm 112:1, 7, "Blessed is the man that feareth the LORD. . . . He shall not be afraid of evil tidings: his heart is fixed, trusting in the LORD."

As you face the year ahead, what fears threaten your peace of mind? Psychologists tell us there are four basic fears that plague people. But the comforting truth is that God, in His Word, provides the solution to each one of them.

11

1. THE FEAR OF WANT

You may be haunted by the fear of want. "What if I lose my job?" you say. "What if I take a cut in salary or I'm sick and cannot work? What if my family is sick or if the bills outstrip my income?" Are these legitimate fears? The Bible says they are not. Why? Because God is the great Provider.

In His great Sermon on the Mount in Matthew 6, Jesus puts the issue plainly. "Wherefore, if God so clothe the grass of the field, which to day is, and to morrow is cast into the oven, shall he not much more clothe you, O ye of little faith?" And then He adds, "Therefore take no thought, saying, What shall we eat? or, What shall we drink? or, Wherewithal shall we be clothed? . . . for your heavenly Father knoweth that ye have need of all these things" (vv. 30-32).

Is Jesus Christ sufficient to supply your needs? Is He faithful? Can you count on His love? The issue is fear or faith. Which will it be? In Psalm 37:25, David says, "I have been young, and now am old; yet have I not seen the righteous forsaken, nor his seed begging bread."

2. THE FEAR OF SUFFERING

Are you facing the fear of suffering? This is the pain of body or of spirit. People can hurt us deeply. We fear sickness or sorrow, loneliness or grief. But can God help you here? Yes, He can and He will! God will not shield you from all suffering, for this is part of life. But He will limit and control it. And He will use it for your good.

Not many years ago, a woman was critically injured in a highway accident. She spent pain-filled months recovering. But in those months, her Christian faith grew and deepened more than in all her previous Christian life. Today she looks back on this experience as the most valuable time of her life.

Suffering may be for the glory of God. It may be for the accomplishing of His purposes. It may be used to refine our character. Whatever the reason, we can trust the God who permits it, rest on His gracious provision, and leave the outcome in His hands.

Often suffering provides an opportunity to know the presence and upholding power of Christ in a way we otherwise would never know it. This was the experience of the apostle Paul. In his second epistle to the Corinthian church, he states that three times he asked God to remove his affliction, and God said, No. Paul goes on to say, "And he said unto me, My grace is sufficient for thee: for my strength is made perfect in weakness. Most gladly therefore will I rather glory in my infirmities, that the power of Christ may rest upon me" (12:9).

We need not fear suffering! God is in control of every circumstance. When He permits it, He will use it for His glory and our good. And He will be with us.

3. THE FEAR OF FAILURE

A very common kind of fear is the fear of failure. Many people are afraid of falling short in school, on the job, in social situations, or in various types of competition. We want to do well. We want to rise to the top. We want to achieve.

This, in fact, is the key to our problem. We fear failure because we rely on ourselves and not the Lord. We want our desires and not His.

God is concerned with faithfulness, obedience, and uprightness of character. If we set our sights on doing God's will, He will help us to succeed. The whole roster of the heroes of faith in Hebrews 11 is made up of men and women who made it the business of their lives not only to believe God, but to do His will.

The opening chapter of the book of Joshua gives us three good rules for success: go forward, trust God, be guided by the Word of God. And God promises, "I will not fail thee, nor forsake thee" (v. 5). We need not fear failure when God is with us.

4. THE FEAR OF DEATH

The greatest fear of all is the fear of death. First Corinthians 15:26 tells us that "the last enemy that shall be destroyed is death." The good news of the Gospel is that Christ has won victory over death, and no man or woman who trusts in Jesus Christ needs to be afraid of death. Jesus says, "Because I live, ye shall live also" (John 14:19).

My friend, do you know that Christ came to deliver you and your loved ones from the fear of death? How? By dying in your place, that you and I might never have to know real death.

We celebrate at Christmas because God became man and was born in a lowly stable. But why did Jesus come? In order to become one of us, to deliver us from death.

The writer of Hebrews tells us that Jesus "took part of the same; that through death he might destroy him that had the power of death, that is, the devil; and deliver them who through fear of death were all their lifetime subject to bondage" (2:14-15).

God has delivered from the fear of death those who trust His Son. That's why David could say, in Psalm 34, "I sought the LORD, and he heard me, and delivered me from all my fears" (v. 4).

CONCLUSION

God delivers us, in a fear-filled world, from all our fears, but only as we believe Him. Will it be fear or faith for you, as you face another year? Will you receive His Son as your Saviour and your Lord?

Fear or faith. You have a choice. God invites you to trust Jesus Christ and be free—free from the power of fear.

TWO

HOW TO HAVE
A HAPPY NEW YEAR

INTRODUCTION

The apostle Paul was an amazing, God-controlled man! He was perhaps the most dynamic Christian to be found in the entire Bible. But successful people, like champions, are generally made, not born. Paul did not become the man he was by accident. He did not, all of a sudden, become a brilliant spokesman for God. At least three words characterize his life, and these same three words will help you discover "how to have a happy new year," as well as a triumphant life.

The three life-changing words that I want to share are *purpose, attitude,* and *motivation.* They are words that describe the writing of Paul in his epistle to the Philippians (Phil 3:10-14).

1. PURPOSE

Whether the apostle Paul was mending tents or writing a letter to an infant church or preaching to a crowd in the market-place, he was driven by one all-consuming, all-controlling, dynamic purpose, and that was "to know God." Paul expressed this purpose in Philippians 3:10, "That I may know him, and the power of his resurrection, and the fellowship of his sufferings, being made conformable unto his death."

In season and out of season, awake or asleep, consciously and subconsciously, Paul relentlessly pursued this dynamic purpose. He possessed a deep desire not merely to know about Jesus Christ but to know Him intimately in all of His glory and humiliation.

Paul's purpose was very much like David of the Old Testament, who prayed, "My soul followeth hard after thee, O God" (Psalm 42:1).

Most of us are familiar with the background of Paul's conversion experience. Acts 7 and 8 relate how Paul, whose pre-Christian name was Saul, persecuted the followers of Jesus. In fact, Paul was responsible for the attack against the church in Jerusalem. In Acts 9, we find him "breathing out threatenings and slaughter" (v. 1) against the disciples of Jesus. In his hands were letters authorizing the arrest of the believers in Damascus. His plan was to bring them bound to Jerusalem.

But as he journeyed to that city, the Lord God of Israel appeared to him. There was a brilliant light and a voice from heaven. Paul knew this was beyond the natural: it was supernatural. In his amazement, he called out, "Who art thou, Lord?" And the Lord said, "I am Jesus whom thou persecutest" (v. 5).

When Paul heard these staggering words, he immediately recognized, for the first time, that Jesus of Nazareth was the Lord God of Israel. Instantly he submitted, calling out, "What wilt thou have me to do?" (v. 6). Paul, the arrester, was arrested by God Almighty. From that very moment on, throughout life, his purpose was "to know God."

Benjamin Disraeli, the former prime minister of Great Britain, said, "The secret of success is *constancy of purpose.*" His emphasis was on the phrase "constancy of purpose." Too often our purpose in life keeps changing from year to year. There is nothing dynamic about it at all. Not so with Paul. His life was a torrent of spiritual desire. His single-mindedness is again expressed in the phrase, "this one thing I do" (Phil 3:13). All his God-given gifts were focused on this one purpose: "that I may know him."

To all those who major in minor concerns, the words of Owen Meredith apply:

> He who seeks all things, wherever he goes
> Only reaps from the hopes which around him he sows
> A harvest of barren regrets.

As a child, I recall having a very interesting jackknife. It had two blades, a gimlet, a corkscrew, a scissors, a can opener, and even a nail file. The whole thing cost a dollar, and it wasn't worth a quarter. The problem was, it was too versatile.

On my desk is a simple reminder: Keep off the detours. I think the apostle Paul felt this way. Humanly speaking, nothing is so powerful in life as single-mindedness.

The apostle James underscored this truth when he warned, "A double minded man is unstable in all his ways" (1:8). It is interesting to realize that the word for worry in the Greek language is *merimino,* which simply means "a divided mind."

Matthew 6:22 states, "If therefore thine eye be single, thy whole body shall be full of light." Jesus was really saying, "Be a one-eyed man."

The picture we are given in Philippians 3 is that of a runner. His eyes are fixed on the goal. As a disciplined athlete, Paul reminds us, "I keep under my body" (1 Cor 9:27). In other words, all the strings of his personality were pulled together in one holy, concerted drive to lay hold of his full potential for the glory of God. My friend, what is the all-consuming, dynamic purpose in your life?

2. ATTITUDE

Attitudes are extremely important. Why? Because attitudes determine actions. They conquer who believe they can. The context of Philippians 3 expresses something of the believing attitude of the apostle Paul. Just notice a few of the powerful, uplifting phrases we find in this passage.

"That I may win Christ" (v. 8).

"That I may know him" (v. 10).

"I follow after" (v. 12).

"Forgetting those things which are behind" (v. 13).

"Reaching forth unto those things which are before" (v. 13).

"I press toward the mark" (v. 14).

Can you feel something of the heartbeat of this aggressive servant of God?

But, you ask, how is it possible, in a chaotic world like ours, to have a believing attitude? How can anyone be that optimistic? I must confess that when I look within at my own heart, I become discouraged. When I look without at our confused world, I am equally overwhelmed. But, when I look up to Jesus Christ, I find a reason for hope and optimism.

The specific word for man in the Greek language is *anthropos,* which is literally, "the up-looking one." The cattle of the field look down. Horses look down. Dogs look down. But men and women who have been born from above are created *to look up,* to fix their eyes on the One who is the source of all hope and strength, the One who is in control of this universe.

The Bible teaches that this kind of attitude begins when one is born anew. This is where it all starts. Salvation is foundational. After we receive Christ, we look up to Him for our every need. First, we're born from above. Then, when we need wisdom, we look up and ask of God (James 1:5).

We are also taught that "every good gift and every perfect gift is from above, and cometh down" (James 1:17). The exhortation of Scripture is "looking unto Jesus."

But you ask, "In a world like ours, how can anyone have a believing attitude?" The answer is found first of all in our new position in Jesus Christ. Romans 5:17 teaches that we can "reign in life" right now, by Jesus Christ. On this particular occasion, the apostle Paul was in a Roman prison awaiting death. Yet enthusiastically he wrote, "Rejoice in the Lord alway: and again I say, Rejoice" (Phil 4:4), and on another occasion, "What shall we then say to these things? If God be for us, who can be against us?" (Rom 8:31). The key to this kind of attitude of faith and victory is in realizing and assuming your position *in* Jesus Christ. Paul's attitude is expressed in that beautiful phrase, "forgetting those things which are behind."

There have been a number of books written in recent years telling how to have a good memory. And I would agree that a good memory is a worthwhile goal. I also firmly believe that it is important to have a good "forgettery." All of us know of people who are defeated in their Christian experience simply because they've never learned how to forget.

A. WE NEED TO FORGET OUR PAST SIN

It is very likely that Paul was guilty of murder. At least he was an accomplice in the death of Stephen. Yet Paul totally repented. After thoroughly dealing with his sin and claiming God's complete forgiveness, he moved on. He forgot those things that were in the past and pressed on in his diligent service for Christ.

B. WE ALSO NEED TO FORGET OUR PAST FAILURES

Why let the blunders of yesterday palsy the hand of today? Perhaps some of you have tried to guide a person to Christ without success, and you have said, "That's not for me." Or you've tried to teach a Sunday school class, and the children were just about impossible, and you said, "That's not for me." Or maybe you tried to pray in public, and the words failed to come, and you said, "That's not for me." But, my friend, it is for me and you. Seek God's cleansing now, and He will enable you.

C. WE NEED TO FORGET OUR PAST SORROWS

All of us, at some time or other, have had our hearts broken. Tears are the common crush of humanity. What are we to do with the sorrowful experiences of life? We must bring them to Jesus. That's what the disciples of John the Baptist did in Matthew 14:12: "And his disciples came, and took up the body, and buried it, and went and told Jesus."

Some of us permit the shattering experiences of life to destroy our usefulness. But that kind of spirit is self-destroying. Let us not say with Naomi, "The Almighty hath dealt very bitterly with me" (Ruth 1:20), but rather, with the hymn writer Johnson Oatman, "Count your many blessings, name them one by one,/ And it will surprise you what the Lord hath done." Always remember that the chisel of the sculptor cuts, but it is to make the image more attractive. The fingers of the potter press in upon the clay, but it is only to make the vessel more beautiful. Let us always remember that every sorrow is the shadow of God's hand and, also, "Whom the Lord loveth he chasteneth" (Heb 12:6).

3. MOTIVATION

In Philippians 3:14 we read, "I press toward the mark for the prize of the high calling of God in Christ Jesus."

Consider the phrase "I press."

The Christian life is not a picnic; it requires discipline plus determination. The words "I press" are strenuous. The picture is that of a runner, straining every muscle, every fiber, every tissue in his forward movement toward the mark.

The Christian life involves work. It is true that we are saved by grace, but let us also remember that "we are his workmanship, created in Christ Jesus unto good works" (Eph 2:10).

True Christianity *demands* discipline plus determination. Just as the runner who is not disciplined will lose the contest, so the believer who is not disciplined will not enjoy success.

The Old Testament tells how flesh hooks were used to adjust the sacrificial offering to the center of the altar. So we also need to take the flesh hooks of discipline and determination and center our lives on the altar of God's will.

When Napoleon became emperor of France, he selected the bee as the emblem of the new France, because it symbolized work and industry. Napoleon wrote, "I love to work. Even when I sleep, I dream about work." He had an insatiable appetite for work. And the program of Christ also demands work. Jesus said, "My Father worketh hitherto, and I work" (John 5:17). "The night cometh, when no man can work" (John 9:4).

But what was Paul's motivation in this particular passage? It is found in Philippians 3:14: "I press toward the mark for the prize of the high calling of God in Christ Jesus." Some scholars believe that the phrase "high calling" refers to the day when believers will be caught away to be with Jesus Christ. They translate the phrase "high calling" as "upward calling."

The context of Philippians 3 also underscores that Paul lived in the light of this grand future event. Paul continues, "For our conversation is in heaven; from whence also we look for the Saviour, the Lord Jesus Christ: who shall change our vile body, that it may be fashioned like unto his glorious body" (Phil 3: 20-21). Paul looked for the coming of the Saviour. This was one of the great motivations of his life. He literally lived in the glow and excitement of the return of Jesus Christ.

CONCLUSION

Some years ago, former president Dwight Eisenhower was in the city of Denver, Colorado. After attending morning worship in his wife's home church, he visited the home of a little boy who was stricken with terminal cancer. The president came unannounced, went up to the little white frame home, and knocked at the door.

The boy's father came to the door and, of course, was overwhelmed by whom he found there. He had been working around the house, and his hair was uncombed and his face unshaven. He was wearing an old T-shirt and torn blue jeans, and there stood President Eisenhower and his assistants.

Well, the presidential party was ushered into the humble home, and a little gift was given to the boy. The president picked him up in his arms and took him out to look at the limousine. In fifteen minutes' time the presidential party was gone. Everyone was excited, and the whole neighborhood was buzzing. That is, everyone was excited except the father; all he could think of was his uncombed hair, bearded face, dirty T-shirt, and torn blue jeans. What a way to meet the president of the United States of America!

One of these days Jesus Christ will come. Are you living in

the excitement of the "upward calling"? The apostle Paul lived in the glow of Christ's return.

One day, according to tradition, the apostle Paul knelt in a Roman arena. In a moment, the sword of Nero crashed on his neck and his head rolled into the dust, and the prize of the high calling of God in Christ was his. Paul was true to his purpose.

For a happy New Year, let me encourage you to resolve to develop a dynamic purpose, a believing attitude, and a heavenly motivation.

THREE

HAVE YOU SEEN
THE KING?

Most people love a parade. Some people will literally wait for hours, just to see some famous person: the president or a royal visitor or even an astronaut. Most processions are soon forgotten.

A few stand out and are remembered because of the occasion and their drama and color. I personally watched the coronation of Queen Elizabeth II, in 1953. Eight perfectly matched horses pulled the royal coach in which Queen Elizabeth II rode from the Tower of London to Westminster Abbey. What an unforgettable procession that was!

A far more humble procession, however, has been remembered for nearly twenty centuries. It is remembered on the day we call Palm Sunday.

Have you ever wondered why this brief and seemingly incidental happening should be recalled each year at Easter? Is it because it opened the events of Passion Week? Or could it be because this event marked a high point in the recognition given Jesus? Let's see what the Bible has to say on this subject.

As we study the Bible, we find that all four gospel writers describe the triumphal entry. John speaks of it briefly in chapter 12, verses 12 to 19. Matthew gives a more full account in chapter 21. In Mark, it is found in chapter 11; in Luke, chapter 19.

You remember what took place. Jesus was about to enter Jerusalem for His final visit. On nearing the city, He sent two disciples with instructions to go to a specific place, where they would find an ass tied with her colt. They were to bring the animal on which no one yet had ridden.

When they brought the colt, they placed their coats upon its back. Then, the record says, "They set Jesus thereon" (Luke 19:

35), and spreading their clothes as a red carpet for Jesus, they moved off toward the city of Jerusalem.

Luke 19:37 and 38 describe what happened next. "And when he was come nigh, even now at the descent of the mount of Olives, the whole multitude of the disciples began to rejoice and praise God with a loud voice for all the mighty works that they had seen; saying, Blessed be the King that cometh in the name of the Lord: peace in heaven, and glory in the highest."

But the acclaim given to Jesus didn't last long. The crowd soon faded, never to rally around Jesus like that again.

Before that happened, however, Luke tells us that there were Pharisees who thought the whole procession was highly improper. "Rebuke your disciples," they urged Him. But Jesus answered, "I tell you that, if these should hold their peace, the stones would immediately cry out" (Luke 19:40).

What was Jesus saying? A careful look at Scripture makes it clear. God's plan for the world is bound up in His promise of a King, a King who can solve the problems of our sick and confused world. That brief recognition two thousand years ago declared that God had kept His promise.

God's King had come. He would not rule right then, for He had a greater purpose. But His eternal Kingdom has been established.

The events of Palm Sunday, then, point to three amazing facts that affect every person born. They are very important and very relevant to you this Palm Sunday. Let me summarize them briefly: (1) God's King *has come* to earth; (2) God's King *will come* to earth again; and (3) God's King *has already begun to reign.*

Each of these facts is true. One does not contradict the other. They are three links in God's eternal purpose. Let me explain.

1. GOD'S KING HAS COME TO EARTH

God's plan for the ages revolves around His King. He was promised to the Jews while the twelve tribes were on the way from Egypt. One of the clearest statements of this promise is in Numbers 24:17 and 19, "There shall come a Star out of Jacob, and a Sceptre shall rise out of Israel.... Out of Jacob shall come he that shall have dominion." This prophecy speaks clearly of a scepter and of power.

During the centuries, the promise was repeated and enlarged. The great King to come would have an everlasting Kingdom. He would rule not only over the Jews but also over the Gentiles. He would bring peace and blessing for which the world has longed since its beginning.

Who was the coming King? The answer is, The One who rode into Jersualem that spring day in what we now describe as the triumphal entry. That procession itself became another proof that Jesus of Nazareth was the long-awaited King.

Five centuries before His birth, the prophet Zechariah had described the entry in minute detail. You'll find the prophecy in Zechariah 9:9: "Rejoice greatly, O daughter of Zion; shout, O daughter of Jerusalem: behold, thy King cometh unto thee: he is just, and having salvation; lowly, and riding upon an ass, and upon a colt the foal of an ass."

Zechariah's statement, of course, was but one of many reminders that Jesus is God's great King, as well as His great Prophet and Priest.

A. HE WAS BORN A KING

True, His birthplace was a stable. But you remember that the wise men who came to find Him asked, "Where is he that is born King of the Jews?" (Matt 2:2).

B. HE LIVED WITH THE AFFAIRS OF A KINGDOM ON HIS MIND

Oh, yes, His way of life was humble, but He had much to say about His Kingdom. Along with John the Baptist, He preached that the Kingdom of heaven was at hand. He warned Nicodemus that, "Except a man be born again, he cannot see the kingdom of God" (John 3:3). He spoke often to His disciples and others, as well, about that Kingdom.

C. He died as a king

True, He was crucified, but as a King. The Roman governor, Pilate, asked Him at His trial, "Are you King of the Jews?" And Jesus' answer was yes (Luke 23:3).

Pilate understood! Do you? At the governor's orders, His cross bore this inscription, in there languages, for all to read: "THIS IS JESUS THE KING OF THE JEWS" (Matt 27:37).

Can you take in what this means? This divided, warring, groping world has had a visit from its King. His time of glory and honor are in the future, but He came.

A week before His death, the little Palm Sunday crowd had seemed to sense it briefly. But he turned aside from reigning then in order to become the Saviour. Have you turned aside from the interests which fill your life to receive His great salvation?

2. God's king is coming again

If it seems incredible, in a day when we hear much of credibility gaps, that God's King is coming again, probably it is only because nothing like it has ever happened before. But may I remind you that nothing like His first coming had ever happened either. Nor did anyone before Jesus overcome death and the grave.

Jesus did die. He was buried, and He rose the third day, leaving an empty tomb! These facts are among the best attested in all history.

Because these things had really taken place and were known to that very generation, the apostle Paul, a few years later, could speak of them boldly on Mars' Hill in Athens. And speak of them he did.

Standing in the intellectual forum of that day, he promised the King's return to judge the earth, as we read in Acts 17. "God . . . commandeth all men every where to repent," he said, "because he hath appointed a day, in the which he will judge the world in righteousness by that man whom he hath ordained."

Then note the final statement: "Whereof he hath given assurance unto all men, in that he hath raised him from the dead" (Acts 17:30-31). The resurrection of Jesus Christ, Paul says, is God's affirmation of a climactic purpose. That purpose is to place His Son on earth to judge and rule.

Again and again the Bible speaks of the King's return. It is the subject of Psalm 2. The King's return is promised by the angels in Acts, chapter 1. Christ Himself spoke of His return in John 14 and in other passages of Scripture. The New Testament contains more than three hundred references to this second coming.

Have you thought of what this means? One of these days you are going to meet eternity's King! You are going to stand before Him. Will He be your Saviour and your King, or will He be your Judge? The Bible warns us plainly that every knee shall bow and "every tongue . . . confess that Jesus Christ is Lord, to the glory of God the Father" (Phil 2:10-11).

3. GOD'S KING HAS ALREADY BEGUN TO REIGN

The Lord Jesus, and others after Him, spoke of the Kingdom more than 125 times in the New Testament. Many of the references are to the glory Kingdom which is to come. But by no means all. Several refer to an unseen Kingdom already in existence.

In Luke 17:20 and 21, the Lord told the Pharisees, "The kingdom of God cometh not with observation . . . for, behold, the kingdom of God is within you," or, "in the midst of you."

What did Jesus mean by that? He was saying that His Kingdom had already begun. Unseen, but very, very real. It is operative in those who discern His lordship and respond to His will.

In the centuries since Christ's ascension, His Kingdom has grown until it circles the globe. Everyone receiving Him as Lord is a citizen of this Kingdom. Thus Colossians 1:13 reminds us

31

that every believer has been delivered from "the power of darkness, and . . . translated . . . into the kingdom of his dear Son."

What does it mean to be in Christ's invisible, yet mighty, Kingdom today? It means all the things that Christians have known and rejoiced in since the day of Pentecost.

It means forgiveness of sins and newfound peace with God.

It means assurance of a home in heaven.

It means being born again and receiving a new heart and mind and will.

It means strength so we can say with Paul, "I can do all things through Christ which strengtheneth me" (Phil 4:13).

It means a special calling to be an ambassador for Christ and for His Gospel.

It means comfort and peace of mind. If you are in Christ's Kingdom, you can know that nothing or no one can separate you from the love of God.

CONCLUSION

Yes, the King is coming. But He has already come, and He is reigning now in the hearts of those who are His own. Have you let Christ place you in His eternal, certain Kingdom? There is no other Kingdom like it. The Word of God says that "of the increase of his government and peace there shall be no end." It will be a kingdom "with judgment and with justice from henceforth even for ever. The zeal of the LORD of hosts will perform this" (Isa 9:7).

There were many that first Palm Sunday in Jerusalem who did not see the King. Have you seen Him now in our day?

FOUR

THE CROSS
OF JESUS CHRIST

Often we divide humanity into many classes: rich and poor, black and white, educated and uneducated. But Jesus drew a line through all these distinctions and divided humanity into just two classes: the unconverted and the converted.

No other division really matters. This is the division that divides! It divides between time and eternity, and Christ and His cross make the difference.

In Matthew 27 we are supplied with some of the details of the crucifixion of Jesus Christ.

1. THE PATH OF THE CROSS

"Then released he Barabbas unto them: and when he had scourged Jesus, he delivered him to be crucified" (Matt 27:26).

Jacob Behemen said, "Man is sometimes like a wolf, cruel and merciless, thirsty for blood; sometimes man is like a dog, snappish, malicious, envious, and grudging as a dog is with a bone; sometimes like a fox, cunning and sly; sometimes like a bear, cruel and ugly; sometimes like a leopard, slippery and fast; sometimes like a snake, sly and fast as zig zag lightning."

We see these very characteristics in the people surrounding the cross. One of the reasons for which Christ came into the world was to give us a new nature in place of our sinful nature. Mankind needs to be changed!

The days prior to the crucifixion portrayed the beastly nature of mankind. The pathway of Jesus grew increasingly dark. The victims of this type of torture were usually chained to a pillar. Rude, barbarous men would surround the prisoner with their whips. The clothing was torn from the body; and the face, pressed hard against the pillar. After firmly tying the one condemned, the soldiers' shameful work began. The scene was dark and ugly. The lashing continued until the arms of the scourgers grew weary, then new recruits took their place, until the entire back of the victim appeared as one big gaping wound. The whips in those days were made of rawhide with slivers of sheep bone and huckle bone inserted.

The physical agony of our Lord's crucifixion was sad enough, but the mental agony was even more profound. The antagonists hurled their words against His kingly position. A threadbare robe was thrown over His beaten back. Then the branches broken from a thorn tree were woven into a crown of thorns and pressed hard upon His head. To complete the image of a mock king, they put in His hands a stick to resemble a kingly scepter. Then they bowed down in mock worship and jeered Him, saying, "Hail, King."

Some slapped Him about the head while others had the arrogance to spit into His face. Still others snatched the reed and beat Him about the head until the thorns dug deep into His forehead.

The gospel reads, "And they stripped him, and put on him a scarlet robe. And when they had platted a crown of thorns, they put it upon his head, and a reed in his right hand: and they bowed the knee before him, and mocked him, saying, Hail, King of the Jews! And they spit upon him, and took the reed, and smote him on the head" (Matt 27:28-30).

These were some of the experiences of Jesus on the path to the cross.

2. THE PLACE OF THE CROSS

"And when they were come unto a place called Golgotha, that is to say, a place of a skull ... they crucified him" (Matt 27: 33-35).

Golgotha. What a frightful name! When interpreted, it

means "the place of a skull." The word *Calvary* comes from the Latin, also meaning "a skull." The place of the crucifixion was skull hill.

This hill was located outside the city of Jerusalem. Foreshadowed in the Old Testament sin offering, Jesus was led outside the city wall, and there He became the final and eternal offering for sin.

Golgotha was the death place. It was also a playground for the vultures, jackals, and hyenas. Yet it was from this hill that there came the hope of the world. From this dark spot flows life, light, and liberty. Around this hill, those of every color, clime, and country clasp hands in the name of Jesus.

"And they crucified him."

You are familiar with the method used. Christ's hands and feet were nailed to the tree. Here was love incarnate, rejected, tortured, and now crucified. The darkest sin of earth was Golgotha. The foulest spot of humanity was Golgotha. The blackest page of history was Golgotha. The place of the crucifixion was "Golgotha."

3. THE PERSON OF THE CROSS

But who was this One so horribly treated? Who was this One who stood the scourging with lamblike patience? Who was this Lamb among wolves? Who was this Dove in the claws of vultures? Who was this One? Who was this One who was to die a criminal's death? My friend, this was none other than the perfect Son of God. This was heaven's "bright and morning star" (Rev 22:16). God Himself said, "This is my beloved Son, in whom I am well pleased" (Matt 3:17).

Rousseau said to Voltaire, "Socrates died like a man, but Jesus died like God." Other men, when crucified, would curse and spit upon the ones who drove in the nails, but Jesus said, "Father, forgive them; for they know not what they do" (Luke 23:34).

Here was heaven's Sun in eclipse, heaven's Lily spotted, heaven's Rose of Sharon dying.

The first Adam was created to be a king. He was given dominion over Eden. God dressed him in a garment of glory. But he sinned. His glory changed to shame and nakedness. His crown degenerated into thorns. He became a slave to sweat, toil, and sin.

The last Adam, Jesus Christ, gathered up the thorns and wove a crown for His head; He wrapped Himself in the robe of mockery and died to restore lost mankind. The God who clothed the valleys and the hills, who hears the raven when it calls, forsook His Son and answered not His cry.

No wonder the earth rocked and reeled in protest. No wonder all the people there on that ugly hill, beholding the things which were done, smote their breasts and returned. No wonder the rocks broke and the earth quaked in view of such divine love. This was Jesus, God's only Son, dying for you and for me.

4. THE PURPOSE OF THE CROSS

The cross shows God pointing His finger at sin and saying, "I hate sin." Sin is a transgression of God's Law. It must be dealt with.

The Bible clearly states that "the wages of sin is death" (Rom 6:23). It also tells us, "The soul that sinneth, it shall die" (Ezek 18:20). Sin is not a minor discord, but a major offense. It is so major that God gave His Son to die for you and me because of it.

What was the purpose of the cross? Matthew records the mockery of the crowd: "He saved others; himself he cannot save" (Matt 27:42). The sarcasm is true! Absolutely true! Jesus died on the cross to redeem others.

God is just. He will never demand two payments for one debt. While on the cross, Jesus said, "It is finished" (John 19:30). What was finished? Throughout His ministry, Jesus told how He would die for the sins of the world, and now that work and purpose was finished.

All the Old Testament offerings found fulfillment in the crucifixion. No more lambs needed to be offered; no more bullocks needed to be bound. Redemption was fulfilled. Redemption was complete as atonement was made through His blood shed on the cross.

American history records the building of a great transcontinental railroad that joined the United States by rail from the Atlantic Ocean to the Pacific Ocean. During its construction, financial failure overtook the promoters, and only with difficulty did they secure the funds to finish the railroad.

There was great enthusiasm when the work was resumed. The day came when the last rail was to be laid on the border between New Mexico and Colorado. It was planned to be a great event. A special order was sent to California for a laurel wood tie, and two silver spikes were ordered, one for Colorado and one for New Mexico. The governor of each state was invited. They were to drive the two silver spikes into the laurel wood tie, thus completing the construction and making a way of transportation from ocean to ocean. As the governors drove the two silver spikes into the laurel tie, the great crowd applauded and a telegraph wire bore the news with a flash to the entire world. It was a great accomplishment!

But there was an infinitely greater day when four spikes were driven, not into a laurel tie, but into the hands and feet of Jesus. They were not spikes of silver, but of iron and steel, and they were driven while heaven, earth, and hell looked on. When the last spike was driven, a shout went up from all creation—the news flashed to the ends of the world—for a way of salvation from earth to heaven had been completed. And Jesus cried, "It is finished."

The way is now open from earth to heaven for you!

Isaiah said, "He hath borne our griefs, and carried our sorrows. . . . He was wounded for our transgressions, he was bruised for our iniquities" (Isa 53:4-5). Peter said, "Who his own self bare our sins in his own body on the tree" (1 Pet 2:24).

CONCLUSION

My friend, our sins nailed Christ to the cross. It is true that Judas betrayed Jesus to Caiaphas. Caiaphas gave Jesus to Pilate. Pilate condemned Him to the cross. But behind Judas, behind Caiaphas, and behind Pilate, were our sins. Our sins crucified Jesus.

Friend, will you see yourself guilty before a holy God? Can you hear the invitation of the crucified, risen, interceding Saviour? At this special season of the year, will you place your trust in the Christ of the cross?

FIVE

THREE ATTITUDES
TOWARD
THE RESURRECTION

INTRODUCTION

A broken man sat in the ruins of his own household. His family had been snatched away by tragedy; his earthly possessions, destroyed. As he viewed the remains of what was once a happy home, he asked this question: "If a man die, shall he live again?" (Job 14:14).

Job's question has been asked repeatedly down through the centuries. Whenever man is faced with death, his thoughts go naturally to the subject of life after death. Death is inescapable. Death comes to us from our streets and highways, and even from our own neighborhoods. Someone has said that in today's society, death has become the most real fact of life. Like it or not, welcome it or dread it, sooner or later we all must die. The Bible states, "It is appointed unto men once to die" (Heb 9:27). No one can avoid death.

For the child of God, death is not the end. It is not a reason for sorrow or despair. Jesus comforted His fearful disciples by saying, "Because I live, ye shall live also" (John 14:19). Only the Christian can look to the future with certainty and a spirit of optimism. Easter speaks of the resurrection of Jesus Christ, and this is our hope.

In Acts 17, we find the apostle Paul waiting for his fellow workers in the godless city of Athens. "Now while Paul waited for them at Athens, his spirit was stirred in him, when he saw the city wholly given to idolatry. Therefore disputed he in the synagogue with the Jews, and with the devout persons, and in the market daily with them that met with him" (vv. 16-17).

As Paul looked around that great city, he was disturbed by the

43

idolatry he encountered. It seemed as if every street corner had an image, and every chariot had an idol. Paul spoke out against this in the synagogues and in the marketplace.

Verse 18 tells us that "certain philosophers of the Epicureans, and of the Stoics, encountered him." They wanted to hear more of this doctrine, "because he preached unto them Jesus, and the resurrection." These very learned men took Paul to the Areopagus on Mars' Hill and said, "Tell us more."

The apostle began by speaking about one God. He continued by telling them that this one God would some day judge the world, and the proof of this judgment to come was the resurrection of Jesus Christ. "Because he hath appointed a day," preached Paul, "in the which he will judge the world in righteousness by that man whom he hath ordained; whereof he hath given assurance unto all men, in that he hath raised him from the dead" (v. 31).

Luke tells us that when Paul spoke about the resurrection, there was a threefold reaction. These three attitudes toward Christ's resurrection are found in verses 32-34: "And when they heard of the resurrection of the dead, some mocked: and others said, We will hear thee again of this matter. So Paul departed from among them. Howbeit certain men clave unto him, and believed."

1. SOME MOCKED

"And when they heard of the resurrection of the dead, some mocked" (Acts 17:32).

The first attitude toward the message of Paul concerning Christ's death, burial, and resurrection was one of mockery. The Scripture simply says that "when they heard of the resurrection . . . some mocked." The Epicureans didn't believe in life after death, and therefore they mocked. The Stoics believed in immortality, but they didn't believe in the literal resurrection of a physical body, and so they mocked.

I used to get very upset when people would mock God. I

44

don't get upset anymore, and I believe this is because I understand the Bible better. I've found that in every age there have been people who mocked God. I think back to the book of Genesis, where society was on an immoral binge. The Lord looked down and recognized that sin had to be dealt with. In Genesis 6:3, the Lord said, "My spirit shall not always strive with man." Society needed to be washed clean. I think it was one of the leaders of the Woodstock Rock Festival who said the whole world needs a big wash, a big scrubdown. I'm sure he was absolutely right.

In the days of Noah, God determined to give the world a big wash by means of a flood. He dealt in judgment and permitted the flood to come. But some people mocked: "Why, Noah, it's never rained. Why waste your time with such foolishness?" However, God had said judgment would come, and it did. And the mockers perished.

Genesis 18 and 19 relate God's judgment upon the wicked city of Sodom. Sodom was so polluted that God cut it off and blotted it out to save the human race from total degeneracy. But when Lot warned his daughters and their families that they must flee, the Scripture says that his sons-in-law mocked him. They looked at their father-in-law and laughed. They thought the old man was out of his mind. Lot's life was so compromising that they couldn't believe he could be that concerned about anyone.

The same was true with Lot's wife. She couldn't make up her mind. She wanted Sodom, and she wanted salvation. She wanted deliverance, and yet she wanted the pleasures that Sodom afforded. God looked at Lot's wife as she delayed, took her hesitation to be no, and rained judgment upon her. She was transformed into a pillar of salt. Yes, the mockers and the delayers described in the Bible met the justice of God. And only those who believed and made a decision were delivered.

Some have always mocked. What about when our Lord was crucified? Instead of a regal throne there was a wooden cross;

45

instead of a kingly diadem, a thorny crown; instead of a regal robe, a tattered shawl; instead of a royal scepter, a stick; instead of a kingdom, the shrunken, narrow dimensions of a borrowed tomb.

Matthew 27 tells a little about that mockery: "Then the soldiers of the governor took Jesus into the common hall, and gathered unto him the whole band of soldiers. And they stripped him, and put on him a scarlet robe. And when they had platted a crown of thorns, they put it upon his head, and a reed in his right hand: and they bowed the knee before him, and mocked him, saying Hail, King of the Jews! And they spit upon him, and took the reed, and smote him on the head" (vv. 27-30).

Yes, they mocked our Lord. You see, the mockers have always been around. I think of what Paul wrote to the Galatian believers: "Be not deceived; God is not mocked: for whatsoever a man soweth, that shall he also reap" (Gal 6:7). Paul is simply saying that you can't mock God and get away with it.

In London, you can take a dog onto a city bus for half fare. One lady, who didn't feel like paying any fare at all, carried her dog in a little cardboard box with air holes in it. She got on and paid her fare, but none for the dog. In essence, she deceived the bus driver, mocked the laws of the transit authority, and thought she was getting away with it.

About three blocks down the road a man got on with a big Airedale dog that he couldn't hide. He paid his fare and the fare for his dog. Because dogs have a way of knowing when other dogs are around, there began a little sniffing and scratching and growling and barking, and soon her secret was out—and so was she. They put her off at the next stop.

When I heard this story, I thought about how people try to deceive, try to get away with things, try to mock the established laws. But God says, "Don't be fooled." He refuses to be mocked. Whatever a person sows, that is exactly what he will reap.

Genesis 37 describes how the sons of Jacob tried to mock him. Jealous of Joseph's dreams, his brothers sold him to a caravan of Ishmaelites. They then took his coat of many colors, dipped it in the blood of slain beasts, brought it to their father, and said, "This have we found: know now whether it be thy son's coat or no" (Gen 37:32). It was nothing more than a deceitful lie that they used to mock their father.

Everything seemed as though they had been quite successful. The years went by, and their sin did not find them out. But as the famine came to the sons of Jacob, they went down to the land of Egypt and came before Joseph. They, of course, didn't recognize their brother; but Joseph, who had risen to a position of authority and power, recognized them. "Joseph said unto his brethren, I am Joseph; doth my father yet live? And his brethren could not answer him; for they were troubled [literally, they were terrified] at his presence" (Gen 45:3). They had mocked their father; they had deceived Jacob; and they thought they had gotten away with it. Time seemed to have covered their sin. But time never covers sin. No one can mock God and get by with it. God will not be mocked; whatever a man sows, that is exactly what he will ultimately reap.

People try to mock God today. Some of the opponents of Christianity say that the resurrection is a deliberate invention of the Church. They say that the resurrection of Jesus is a lie. This of course, is not valid in view of the great number of witnesses to it. Why, in A.D. 56, Paul says there were 500 original witnesses of the resurrected Lord. We also must remember that the early Scripture record went out to the known world with the collective authority of the whole Church. These witnesses were men of exceptional character. They gave to the world the highest moral and ethical teaching ever known. They lived what they taught, and their opponents knew it. And how do you explain the fantastic change which occurred in these men? Could a deliberate lie produce such transforming results?

Yes, there are some who mock today. They mock by saying that the resurrection of Christ was a spiritual resurrection. But a spirit is intangible. Whoever heard of a spirit rising?

47

Some mock by saying that the disciples stole the body of Jesus. They say that Matthew, Mark, Luke, John, Peter, and Paul lied; they invented a fabrication. But those men thought it was wrong to lie. Can you believe that they would concoct a story and then have the gall to circulate the lie? If so, what did they do with the body of Jesus? And why were they willing to suffer martyrdom? For what? For a lie?

Someone might say, "The disciples didn't steal the body. The local authorities did." Well, then, why didn't they produce it when Peter stood and preached about the resurrection of Christ? When thousands were believing and the Church was multiplying greatly, why didn't the authorities produce His body then?

Some modern writers mock by saying that Jesus never died at all. The author of *The Passover Plot,* a recent best-seller, suggests that Jesus really didn't die, but fainted or swooned, and was then revived as He lay in the cold tomb. But tell me, how could He, in that wounded condition, roll away the stone? And tell me, what happened to the soldiers who guarded that sepulcher? Why didn't they stop Him? How far could He walk on wounded feet? Where did He go from there? Even some skeptics agree that this is absolutely absurd.

Peter tells us that in the last days there will be mockers who will say, "Where is the promise of his coming?" (2 Pet 3:4). As Paul stood on Mars' Hill and spoke about Christ's resurrection, they looked and laughed. Some mocked the message of the resurrection.

2. SOME DELAYED

"And others said, We will hear thee again of this matter" (Acts 17:32).

The second attitude toward the resurrection is that of delay. I don't think there are many who would mock God or who would mock Christ's death, burial, and resurrection. But I am positive that there are many who would and do take this second attitude.

I think of the delay of Pharaoh. Moses went to the king and

48

said, "Let my people go." Pharaoh said, "Look, I don't know your Jehovah. I know Ra, but I don't know Jehovah. I will not let Israel go." So God sent judgment.

In the midst of each judgment, Pharaoh said, "Moses, ask your God to take this plague away." And each time Moses would say, "Tell me, Pharaoh, when will you let Israel go?" Each time Pharaoh answered, "I'll let Israel go tomorrow" (Exod 8:10, author's paraphrase). At first his neck was hard, then his heart was hard, and, finally, when he pursued the children of Israel across the Red Sea, God smote him with sudden death because he hardened his will and his heart against the warnings of God. He kept delaying until "tomorrow."

Tomorrow looks so innocent; it sounds so innocent; but it isn't innocent. The men of Athens listened to Paul and said, "Not now. We'll hear more about this matter later." They delayed.

Oh, how tragic it is to say *tomorrow* when God says *today*. Proverbs 27:1 declares, "Boast not thyself of to morrow; for thou knowest not what a day may bring forth." I have found that people who intend to repent at twelve, often die at eleven. Don't count on tomorrow!

James 4:13-14 declares, "Go to now, ye that say, To day or to morrow we will go into such a city, and continue there a year, and buy and sell, and get gain: whereas ye know not what shall be on the morrow. For what is your life? It is even a vapor, that appeareth for a little time, and then vanisheth away."

Waiting for tomorrow is a mistake, because life is like a vapor. It's like an arrow speeding for a target, like an eagle chasing its prey, like a leaf falling to the ground, like a weaver's shuttle that moves so fast the eye cannot distinguish movement. The life of an individual is so brief that the wood of the cradle rubs against the marble of the tomb. It is presumptuous to say we'll wait for tomorrow. God says the only time we can count on is right now.

I think of a couple who were attending meetings a few years ago. Night after night an elderly, godly man lovingly, tenderly, tactfully, tried to persuade them to receive Christ. Each night the husband would say, "Not tonight, but tomorrow." He left the meetings without Christ, characterized by indecision and delay. One day, before he went to work, he said to his wife, "Honey, never since that meeting have I had the slightest urge, the slightest tendency to repent and get right with God." They determined that they would make time to think about their souls' salvation. But that day at work an explosion snuffed out that young man's life. He said "tomorrow" when God said "today."

Edgar Guest penned these words:

> He was going to be all that a mortal should be
>   Tomorrow.
> No one should be kinder or braver than he
>   Tomorrow. . . .
> Each morning he stacked up the letters he'd write
>   Tomorrow. . . .
> The greatest of workers this man would have been
>   Tomorrow.
> The world would have known him, had he ever seen
>   Tomorrow.
> But the fact is he died and he faded from view,
> And all that he left here when living was through
> Was a mountain of things he intended to do
>   Tomorrow.[1]

I have found that the road marked tomorrow leads to the town called never. Tomorrow is the door that's been bolted, barred, boarded; it shuts people out from the mercy and grace of God. Tomorrow is not God's time; it is Satan's time. I would suggest you write that letter today, or make that phone call today. I would suggest that if you're not right with a fellow believer, you get right today. I suggest that you make restitution today. I would suggest that if a step of obedience is needed, you take that step. I would suggest that if you have never repented and received Christ, you receive Christ while it is yet day. He-

---

1. Reprinted from *Collected Verse of Edgar A. Guest* by Edgar A. Guest, copyright 1934 by the Reilly and Lee Company, a division of the Henry Regnery Company, Chicago. Used by permission.

brews 2:3 asks, "How shall we escape, if we neglect so great salvation?"

Several years ago our family visited Niagara Falls. It was spring, and ice was rushing down the river. As I viewed the large blocks of ice flowing toward the falls, I could see that there were carcasses of fish imbedded in the ice. Gulls by the score were riding down the river feeding on the fish. As they came to the brink of the falls, their wings would go out, and they would escape from the falls.

I watched one gull which seemed to delay and wondered when it would leave. It was engrossed in the carcass of a fish, and when it finally came to the brink of the falls, out went its powerful wings. The bird flapped and flapped and even lifted the ice out of the water, and I thought it would escape. But it had delayed too long so that its claws had frozen in the ice. The weight of the ice was too great, and the gull plunged into the abyss. Oh the danger of delay.

No one has ever drifted to God. You don't drift to heaven. You must make an intelligent, active decision to move in the direction of heaven. You can drift from faith to reason and from reason to the senses and from the senses to animalism, but no one ever drifts toward God. Paul was drifting into a life of violence until one day, on the Damascus road, Christ arrested him and gave him the power he needed to go a new direction.

You say you don't have the power to stick by a decision. You don't have the power to live the life. You're afraid you can't last if you make a decision. Christ who saves is the One who empowers, and He will give you what you are lacking.

Matthew 25 speaks about the wise and foolish virgins. The five foolish ones were not anti-God; they were not antibridegroom. They just neglected to get oil. They were unprepared. In Matthew 25:10 we read, "And while they went to buy, the bridegroom came; and they that were ready went in with him to the marriage: and the door was shut."

The five foolish virgins were not God-rejecters. They were delayers. They were procrastinators. They failed to make a decision. Clocks that are not wound eventually refuse to tell time; white fences that are not cared for become black fences; water that is undisturbed develops a green color and a foul odor. Neglect alone will do it. Neglect will damn you.

The Bible asks the question, How do you imagine you will escape if you neglect so great salvation offered by a loving, holy God?

3. SOME BELIEVED

"Howbeit certain men clave unto him, and believed" (Acts 17:34).

The third atttiude is expressed in verse 34: "Howbeit certain men clave unto him, and believed." What is it to believe? First of all, it is to confess your sins. The word *confess* means to agree. It's to come to the Lord and say, "Lord, You're right and I am wrong." If you're a Christian out of fellowship, it's to say, "Lord, I'm out of fellowship." If you've never received Jesus Christ, it's to say, "Lord, I'm sinful, I'm dead spiritually, and I admit my need of forgiveness. I'm incomplete. I've come short of the glory of God." To believe is to acknowledge your need and to acknowledge Jesus Christ as the only One to meet that need.

Luke says that those who believed were "Dionysius the Areopagite, and a woman named Damaris, and others with them" (v. 34). Some mocked, some delayed, and some believed.

In Athens, to be a believer was to be in the definite minority. Yet these went up to Paul and held on to him and said, "Paul, we're with you. We believe, and we're not ashamed. We believe, and we'll openly acknowledge Jesus Christ. In spite of all this heathen worship, we believe. You can count on us." They held on to Paul; they clave unto him. Theirs was a public profession of faith in Christ.

Just suppose that after having discovered the final phase of the polio vaccine, Dr. Jonas Salk had said, "I'm not going to let anyone use this new discovery. I'll not share my remedy." You say, "That's inhuman." I say that it is equally inhuman to receive, to believe, to accept God's gift of salvation and to keep it to yourself. The Bible says, "Whosoever therefore shall confess me before men, him will I confess also before my Father which is in heaven" (Matt 10:32).

When Nicodemus and Joseph of Arimathea saw Jesus die, their hearts were moved, and they openly begged His body and gave Him a proper burial. It took His death to turn them from secret believers to open believers. Then they identified themselves with the followers of Jesus Christ. Have you believed? Have you publicly professed your faith?

CONCLUSION

The football game was over. Four fellows piled into their car and started home. As they drove, they drank. They drove along the road ignoring all of the highway warnings. They passed signs that said, "Five miles ahead—Bridge Out"; "Four miles ahead—Bridge Out"; "Three miles ahead—Bridge Out." "One mile ahead—Bridge Out"; "500 yards ahead—Bridge Out." They drank and drove. They came to a black and white barricade with flashing lights, but in their drunkenness they drove through the barricade and into the icy water of the river. All four perished that Saturday afternoon.

Along the road of your life, God has placed many warnings. The church, a praying neighbor, a teacher, a book, a conference, some pastor or teacher or evangelist you've heard on TV. All along the road of your life there has been warning after warning after warning after warning. Finally, at the end of your life, there's a barricade, the barricade of the cross. If you perish, it's because you've neglected every kindness of God. It's because you have walked over every mercy of God. If you go out of this life without Christ, eventually you take the barricade of the cross and trample it underfoot. In spite of all that God has done, you neglect so great salvation.

Some mocked. Some delayed. But some believed.

53

SIX

THE GOOD NEWS OF EASTER

INTRODUCTION

Around the globe, on hundreds of fronts, medicine is waging a war on sickness and death. In 1967, in Cape Town, Africa, Dr. Christian Barnard completed the world's first heart transplant. The patient, a victim of advanced heart disease, lived only eighteen days. A second transplant attempt was unsuccessful, but a third man was operated on again in Cape Town and lived for nineteen months before succumbing to pneumonia. Since then, hundreds of heart transplants have been performed. Other remarkable advances are being made in diagnosis, medicine, and techniques of surgery.

In London, England, Dr. Alexander Comfort, director of Research for the Aging at University College, says, "We hope to find a technique for interfering with human aging within the next four or five years—not for stopping the process but for slowing it down."

Yes, science has made much progress, but death is still our greatest enemy. In a very real sense, we begin to die the moment we are born. Death is, for everyone, an inescapable fact of life.

But there is hope! Nearly two thousand years ago, a body lay in a tomb and was raised to life. And because Jesus Christ rose, you, too, can know the certainty of resurrection. This is the good news of Easter and the basic message of the Gospel, as Paul writes in 1 Corinthians 15:3-4: "For I delivered unto you first of all that which I also received." This is assurance, this is certainty, passed to us through the Word of God. Paul continues, "How that Christ died for our sins according to the scriptures; and that he was buried, and that he rose again the third day."

These are facts. Not suppositions. Though Jesus Christ rose

nearly two thousand years ago, the details of this great event are among the best attested in all history. True, we are far removed in time and distance, but we have much reliable evidence from a number of witnesses. Matthew, Mark, Luke, John, the two followers who met Jesus on the Emmaus road, Thomas, the other disciples, and many others, all tell us Jesus died and rose again!

The enemies of Jesus would have given their very lives for one single piece of evidence to show that a resurrection had not taken place. But they found none, absolutely none.

On the other hand, proofs of the resurrection are overwhelming. A recent book, *Evidence That Demands a Verdict,* by Josh McDowell, devotes no fewer than eighty-eight pages to this important subject. Proof after proof is cited confirming the fact that Christ arose and left an empty tomb.

Have you ever faced this fact and what it means to you? Let me set before you three phases of the evidence, just three of many, which no thinking person can ignore.

1. THE FACTS OF JESUS' DEATH

First, there is the fact that Jesus really died. That was the purpose of crucifixion, and the Roman soldiers were efficient.

After a night of exhaustion and abuse, He was scourged: lashed with a whip to which were fastened long pieces of bone and metal. An early Church historian says that in such scourgings, the sufferer's veins were laid bare and that "the very muscles, sinews and bowels were open to exposure." Hebrew law limited the number of strokes to forty, but the Romans had no such limitation.

Christ's sufferings on the cross are beyond our understanding. After six hours of indescribable agony, the gospels tell us, He died. At the end of the day, when Roman soldiers came to break the victims' legs, they found Him already dead. When a Roman soldier pierced His side with a spear, there flowed out blood and water. This suggests not only death by crucifixion, but rupture of the heart. Some have tried to argue that Jesus only fainted, but remember, He was certified as dead before His body was released for burial.

Our Lord's body was then wrapped in spices—John says about one hundred pounds—and left in the grave. The tomb was closed with a huge stone. It would take several men to move it. It was sealed with the Roman seal so that any person removing it would have been guilty of crime against the Roman government. As if all this were not enough, the tomb was guarded, not by one, but by several professional soldiers.

But by Easter morning the stone had been rolled away. Only the body windings were left, collapsed and empty, inside the tomb.

All Jerusalem knew these facts, but the only answer offered was a weak and absurd rumor that the soldiers had been asleep and the disciples had stolen Jesus' body.

2. THE FACT THAT JESUS WAS SEEN ALIVE BY MANY DIFFERENT PEOPLE

There is also the fact that Jesus was seen alive by different people. The list is long: Mary Magdalene, the two Marys together, Simon Peter, and two believers on the road to Emmaus. He also appeared to the disciples in the upper room when Thomas was absent and again when he was present. He met the disciples by the Sea of Tiberias. Think of this a moment. Could all these people have been deceived?

There were other meetings, too. Matthew tells of one with the disciples in Galilee, and Paul, in 1 Corinthians 15, records His appearing to more than five hundred believers at once (v. 6), and later to James (v. 7). Finally, He appeared to the disciples on the day that He went back to heaven.

Jesus talked with them. He ate food. He let them see and touch His hands and feet and side. In each case, the impression was the same. The Jesus who had been dead was now alive.

The facts themselves prove that Christ rose from the dead. The testimony of those who saw Him prove it, but there is

57

another important proof. The believers who saw the risen Christ were changed.

3. THE FACT THAT THE BELIEVERS WHO SAW THE RISEN CHRIST WERE CHANGED

They were convinced of Jesus' resurrection. These were the very men who were on the scene. Days earlier they were crushed, defeated, discouraged, and afraid. Then, a total change came over them! In the face of opposition and almost certain death, they went out with boldness to preach a living Christ everywhere. Why? Because they knew He was alive!

CONCLUSION

Yes, Jesus Christ lives! Jesus Christ rose from the grave and lives today. You can anchor your faith to this tremendous fact. But the Good News of Easter is also something more. It is the assurance that every Christian who dies will be raised up one day, even as Christ Himself was raised.

That wonderful resurrection chapter, 1 Corinthians 15, makes this very clear. Listen to these words of assurance. "But now is Christ risen from the dead, and become the firstfruits of them that slept" (v. 20).

What are the firstfruits? The Jews knew the answer well because of their yearly feast. The firstfruits are the first sheaves of grain, the first clusters of grapes or ears of corn, in the season's harvest. They are the first visible tokens of the harvest yet to come.

The risen Christ is the first of thousands upon thousands whom God will raise from the dead because Jesus Christ was raised for us. "Because I live," Jesus told His disciples in John 14:19, "ye shall live also."

Year after year, thousands of visitors go to Forest Lawn Memorial Park in Glendale, California, to see two huge paintings. One pictures the crucifixion. The other shows the artist's concept of the outcome of Christ's resurrection. A figure in white, emerging from a tomb, depicts the risen Saviour. Behind Him is a great procession which fades into the misty distance. This is the throng of believers through the ages whose bodies will be raised like His because they have trusted Jesus.

What really happens, then, when a Christian dies? First, the spirit goes at once to be with Christ. The Bible tells us plainly that "to be absent from the body" is "to be present with the Lord" (2 Cor 5:8). Paul reminds us that this will be "far better" (Phil 1:23) than our present life.

But our bodies will not remain in the grave. At the great resurrection morning, we will respond, like Lazarus, to the voice of Christ. This is the promise of 1 Thessalonians 4:16-17: "For the Lord himself shall descend from heaven with a shout, with the voice of the archangel, and with the trump of God: and the dead in Christ shall rise first: then we which are alive and remain [those living at the time of the rapture] shall be caught up together with them in the clouds, to meet the Lord in the air: and so shall we ever be with the Lord."

Think of it! If you pass through the door of death as a true believer, Jesus Christ will one day raise your body.

We see a picture of resurrection each time we watch a seedling sprout and grow. The seed died first, time passed, and then God created life anew in the form and image of the seed that died.

If a loved one trusted Christ, we need not fear as we lay that body in the grave. The loved one will be raised in a glorious resurrection body—raised in the likeness we have known so well.

My friend, are you in bondage to the fear of death today? Jesus died and rose again to set you free. The Good News of Easter Sunday is not only that Jesus arose from the dead, not only that every Christian can experience this same mighty resurrection. It is that you have a choice to make! Christ invites you to share the promise and the reality of resurrection. In John 6:40, He says, "And this is the will of him that sent me, that every one which seeth the Son, and believeth on him, may have everlasting life." And then He adds, "And I will raise him up at the last day."

Friend, you must have Christ! No power within you can hope to overcome the bonds of death. But Jesus can, and He promises to do so. Will you put your trust in Him?

Every day, nearly half a million Americans travel by air across this country. No one has ever personally learned to overcome the hard, cold law of gravity. But they have learned a better way. One by one, they commit themselves to airliners that are made to fly. And they're carried safely to their destinations.

The Bible says that those who trust Christ are "in" Him. Trust the One who died for your sins, who rose again to give you hope and certainty of life, and He will forgive your sins. He will give you eternal life and clothe you with a resurrection body. Receive Him now and you, too, will know the Good News of Easter.

SEVEN

A SUCCESSFUL MOTHER

INTRODUCTION

We are living in a changing world! Motherhood, the American flag, and apple pie are three things known for their stability and national appeal. Today, however, the price of apples is inflated, the flag is at times mistreated, and even motherhood is abused.

Napoleon once said, "Let France have good mothers and she will have good sons." Today, more than ever, we need mothers of character, mothers who will nurture their children in the ways of God. The successful mother is the key to a successful home and nation.

Several years ago, a nationwide survey was conducted by the University of Michigan. Thousands of girls between the ages of eleven and eighteen were questioned regarding their personal and social interests. When asked what they would like to do when they grew up, 80 percent of the girls expressed a desire to someday be just like their mother.

It has been said that no other force in the life of a child is as strong an influence as is his mother. This year, as each year, a special day has been officially designated as Mother's Day, the day we honor America's fifty million mothers.

Down through the centuries, the mother has been a stabilizing factor in the shaping of history. "The future destiny of the child," said Napoleon, "is always the work of the mother."

Theodore Roosevelt put it this way: "The mother is the one supreme asset of the national life. She is more important, by far, than the successful statesman, businessman, artist or scientist."

Many famous men have been greatly influenced by their

63

mothers. George Washington's mother was a patriotic and religious woman. Her son became the father of his country. Lord Bacon's mother was a woman of superior intelligence and deep piety. The mother of Patrick Henry was known for her remarkable conversational ability. Sir Walter Scott's mother was a great lover of poetry and literature.

In contrast, Byron's mother was proud, contentious, and violent. And Nero's mother was greedy, lustful, and a murderess. Without a doubt, a mother influences her children for either good or evil.

Susannah Wesley was a great Christian mother. Despite the fact that she had nineteen children, she found time to give each child an hour's religious instruction each week. She taught her children to love God and to honor the Bible. One of her sons, John Wesley, became the founder of Methodism.

In each of these examples, some of the prominent traits of the mother were passed on to the child.

After becoming president, Abraham Lincoln generously said, "All that I am, or can become, I owe to my angel mother." That's a great tribute!

An older mother once tried to explain to me why her son's marriage had failed and he had committed suicide. "Pastor," she said, "our home was a broken home, and the old saying is true, 'There are few unbroken eggs in a broken nest.'"

If ever there was a need for godly mothers, it is today.

In 1 Samuel 1, we see a beautiful portrait of a woman who honored God. Hannah of Ephraim lived in a day when the nation of Israel was in a deplorable state. The condition of that time closely resembles the corrupt society of today. The nation's leaders had failed. Gideon and Samson were nothing more than memories. Patriotism had vanished, and ideals were low. The heroes were all dead, and the prophets were unborn. The nation was in a cowardly condition. A spiritual revival was desperately needed.

The Scriptures tell us that Hannah came from a little town

called Ramathiam-zophim. It was just a wide spot in the road. The biggest thing about it was its name. And yet in this obscure little village, God had a mother, and He would eventually have His prophet.

The conditions were much the same in the year 1483. Who would have dreamed, in the little town of Eisleben, that the hope of the Reformation would be born in a miner's hut, and that God was waiting for a husky boy named Martin Luther to grow up and steer the world back to the Word of God.

God often uses the little people of this world to bring about His divine purpose. So it was with Hannah of Ramathiam-zophim.

1. HANNAH'S PRAYER

Hannah, the wife of Elkanah, was a woman with great sorrow. She had been denied that which was the crowning glory of every Hebrew woman: the privilege of motherhood.

For years Hannah had prayed for a son. She had longed to take him with her to Shiloh on the yearly pilgrimage of worship. And now, still with no child, her disappointment seemed more than she could bear.

The Scriptures tell us that she was deeply disturbed. "She was in bitterness of soul, and prayed unto the LORD, and wept sore" (1 Sam 1:10). As God listened to that prayer, He seemed to say, "I have found a concerned mother, and now I shall have a dedicated servant."

Hannah prayed to the Lord, and the Lord heard her prayer! She was just a simple woman; she was not educated; her clothing was very plain; and yet God heard her prayers.

Hannah's name would not be found among the wealthy or elite. She would not have made the society pages, but somehow she made the V.I.P. list of heaven.

2. HANNAH'S ANSWER

Hannah was a praying mother! And the Bible tells us that

the Lord heard her prayer. "It came to pass . . . that she bare a son, and called his name Samuel" (v. 20).

May I encourage you, dear mother, to be a praying mother. Your prayer life is the foundation of a godly home. Hannah was a praying mother. She prayed for a son, and God heard her. She promised God that if He would bless her with a child, she would give him back to God. She would train him in the way of the Lord.

The greatest sermon our children will ever hear is our lives. We are examples. "Apples do not fall far from the trees." What is your attitude? Is it small or big, stingy or generous? Are you negative or positive, critical or complimentary, godly or ungodly? Hannah had an attitude of praise! She taught her child to love and honor God.

The Jewish Talmud asks the question, "Who is best taught?" It then answers, "He that is taught of his mother."

Moses said, concerning the Scriptures, "Thou shalt teach them diligently unto thy children, and shalt talk of them when thou sittest in thine house, and when thou walkest by the way, and when thou liest down, and when thou risest up" (Deut 6:7). Morning, noon, or night, Moses said, "Teach God's Word." When you are sitting, walking, going to bed, getting up, whatever you are doing, stress God's Word.

A visiting friend found a young mother sitting with her baby on her lap and holding her Bible in her hand. She asked, "Are you reading the Bible to your baby?" The mother replied, "Yes." The visitor said, "Surely you do not think he understands it?" "No," said the mother, "he does not understand it now, but I want his earliest memory to be that of seeing and hearing God's Word."

The Sunday school will train the child; the church will provide Christian nurture; but nothing can take the place of the home in providing spiritual leadership.

3. Hannah's Commitment

Hannah had made a vow to the Lord. Within a few short years, the time came for her to give Samuel back to God. She would travel to Shiloh and leave Samuel at the tabernacle. He would become a servant of Jehovah.

Hannah was made of the material of which martyrs are made. I can see her gathering her clothing, assembling all the provisions for the journey. Her heart was very heavy. She occasionally glanced at Samuel and listened to his childish words. She would miss him dearly.

At last they made the journey. Arriving at the house of the Lord, an attendant greeted them and took little Samuel and his bundle of clothes. The inevitable moment had arrived. Hannah gave her boy one last hug and turned to walk the lonely road homeward.

In 1 Samuel 1:28, Hannah's words were: "Therefore also I have lent him to the LORD; as long as he liveth he shall be lent to the LORD." What a beautiful picture of a mother dedicated to God! Hannah gave her boy to the Lord. Not to business, not to society, not even to her country. She gave him to God!

Conclusion

Many great men and women of God are serving Christ today not because of their great talent or ability but because they had a mother who gave them to God. Augustine, the great Church Father and theologian, had a mother who devoted her life to his Christian upbringing and his conversion to Christ. In his early years, it would have appeared that her earnest efforts were all for nought. Augustine lived in sin and immorality; he flaunted all moral restraint and actively rebelled against God. But one day he was brought to his senses; he remembered his praying mother; and he repented of his sins. He was gloriously saved and became a champion of the Christian faith.

There once was a young lady who ignored the claims of Jesus Christ. She laughed at her mother's prayers and turned her back upon her mother's God. She seemingly was headed in the wrong direction. There came a day, however, when she was moved to pen these words:

I grieved my Lord from day to day,
I scorned His love so full and free.
And though I wandered far away,
My mother's prayers have followed me.

I'm coming home, I'm coming home,
To live my wasted life anew,
For mother's prayers have followed me,
Have followed me the whole world through.[1]

Perhaps you had a Christian mother who prayed for you. She prayed for many years, but as yet you have not surrendered. You have refused to yield your life to Jesus Christ. Perhaps your mother has gone on to heaven. She is there waiting for you right now. Won't you receive Christ today? Jesus says, "Behold, I stand at the door, and knock: if any man hear my voice, and open the door, I will come in" (Rev 3:20).

---

1. Lizzie DeArmond, "Mother's Prayers Have Followed Me," copyright 1912 by B. D. Ackley. © Ren. 1940 The Rodeheaver Co., owner. Used by permission.

EIGHT

MARY, THE MOTHER OF JESUS

Have you ever wondered why God chose Mary to be the mother of Jesus? Mary was a very unique person, the only one among millions of women to be selected as God's instrument for bringing His Son into the world. She is truly unique!

But why was Mary blessed of God? Why was she so highly favored? Notice five important reasons.

1. MARY WAS PURE

The village of Nazareth, where Mary lived and grew up, lay in the path of caravans going from Capernaum to the seaports. As in every generation, there were women in that town who became involved with the traveling men. But not so with Mary! Mary was pure!

Of course, there could not have been any unfaithfulness in Mary. Otherwise God could not have chosen her. The words that came to her from Gabriel that day echoed God's full approval: "And the angel said unto her, Fear not, Mary: for thou hast found favour with God. And, behold, thou shalt conceive in thy womb, and bring forth a son, and shalt call his name JESUS. He shall be great, and shall be called the Son of the Highest: and the Lord God shall give unto him the throne of his father David: and he shall reign over the house of Jacob for ever; and of his kingdom there shall be no end" (Luke 1:30-33).

Some of the great masterpieces of art picture the angel announcing this message to Mary and presenting her with a branch of lily. The lily is a symbol of Mary's purity.

There are those today who reject that Mary was a virgin.

71

They attempt to do away with the supernatural reality of Christ's birth by suggesting Jesus was born of a natural, human union. But to deny the virgin birth of Jesus is to plainly call God a liar.

Centuries before the angel appeared to Mary, God's prophet Isaiah wrote these words: "Therefore the Lord himself shall give you a sign; Behold, a virgin shall conceive, and bear a son, and shall call his name Immanuel" (Isa 7:14).

God, through His Word, required that Mary be a virgin, pure and holy.

What is more, to reject the virgin birth is to label Mary as immoral. The Bible clearly points out that she and Joseph, to whom she was betrothed, had not yet come together. Either Mary was pure, or else she was a woman with few morals at all.

Without the virgin birth, we have an impure Mary. Without the virgin birth, we have a human Jesus and a faulty Bible. But with the virgin birth, we have Jesus Christ, Immanuel, God with us!

When Mary received the angel's announcement, she was overwhelmed. "How shall this be, seeing I know not a man?" she exclaimed (Luke 1:34). But the angel reassured her, "The Holy Ghost shall come upon thee, and the power of the Highest shall overshadow thee: therefore also that holy thing which shall be born of thee shall be called the Son of God" (Luke 1:35).

Then the angel gave more proof to Mary that her child would really be without a human father. What was this proof? "And, behold, thy cousin Elisabeth, she hath also conceived a son in her old age; and this is the sixth month with her, who was called barren. For with God nothing shall be impossible" (Luke 1:36-37).

If God could do this for Elisabeth, then He could do anything. Mary went to visit her cousin. When Mary and Elisabeth met, Elisabeth knew immediately that Mary was the woman of God's own choosing. She greeted her as the mother of her Lord, with great happiness.

Yes, Mary was pure. As God's chosen instrument, she is to be recognized for the special role she played in the coming of the Messiah.

2. MARY WAS SUBMISSIVE

When the angel finished his startling announcement that Mary was to be the mother of the Messiah, Mary beautifully responded, "Behold the handmaid of the Lord; be it unto me according to thy word" (Luke 1:38).

"Lord, I'm Your servant. Whatever You want, I want. May it happen to me according to Your word." What submission! Mary could have hesitated or even rebelled. She could have said, "I'm so unworthy. I can never be the one." Or she could have reasoned, "We have no royal home for the Son of the Highest. He should have angelic nurses to care for Him. Please don't count on me."

But she didn't. In fact, Mary was willing even to lose her beloved Joseph in order to fulfill God's plan. I'm sure in Mary's mind there were many questions: "What will I tell people since I have no husband? And what will I tell Joseph, the man I'm engaged to, the man I'm planning to marry?" How overwhelmed and confused she must have been.

But also think of what Joseph must have felt. When he heard about Mary, I'm sure he was disturbed by doubt. Yes, disturbed and heartsick. Mary had not told him how she had come to be in this condition. From Matthew's account, we learn that Joseph was understandably upset.

"Then Joseph . . . being a just man, and not willing to make her [Mary] a publick example, was minded to put her away privily. But while he thought on these things, behold, the angel of the Lord appeared unto him in a dream, saying, Joseph, thou son of David, fear not to take unto thee Mary thy wife: for that which is conceived in her is of the Holy Ghost" (Matt 1:19-20).

Mary had been willing to suffer all the shame and reproach that would result from her condition. Why? Because she totally believed God and knew that it was His supernatural hand at work within her. And the Lord rewarded Mary's submissiveness by sending an angel to Joseph.

Yes, let's recognize Mary for her purity and for her spirit of submissiveness.

3. MARY KNEW HER BIBLE

She loved the Word of God. Although she was very young, possibly still in her teens, Mary was a devout person. She knew the Scriptures well. She had studied the Law and the prophets.

Her song, or what we often call "The Magnificat," refers to portions of Scripture taken from 1 Samuel, the Psalms, Isaiah, Micah, and Exodus. It is a very beautiful passage. Part of it is found in Luke 1:46-49:

"And Mary said, My soul doth magnify the Lord, and my spirit hath rejoiced in God my Saviour. For he hath regarded the low estate of his handmaiden: for, behold, from henceforth all generations shall call me blessed. For he that is mighty hath done to me great things; and holy is his name."

It is true that Mary could have uttered these words under divine inspiration, possibly without any forethought on her part, but usually God uses the talent He has already bestowed.

Mary was familiar with the Word of God. And what she had studied and pondered in her heart broke out in glorious praise to her Lord. Mary saturated her life with the Scriptures.

4. MARY WAS INDUSTRIOUS

"Who can find a virtuous woman?" asks the writer of Proverbs, "for her price is far above rubies" (31:10). She then is described as one who "worketh willingly with her hands" (v. 13).

"She is like the merchants' ships; she bringeth her food from afar" (v. 14).

"She riseth also while it is yet night, and giveth meat to her household, and a portion to her maidens" (v. 15).

"She layeth her hands to the spindle" (v. 19).

"She stretcheth out her hand to the poor; yea, she reacheth forth her hands to the needy" (v. 20).

"Strength and honour are her clothing; and she shall rejoice in time to come" (v. 25).

These words could well describe young Mary. Apparently neither she nor Joseph came from a wealthy home. There was always much hard work to be done. Mary knew what it was to toil in the field, to grind corn, to wash her laundry at the well, and to carry water.

The usual pictures we see of Mary are probably quite different from the hardworking homemaker she really was. Mary was pure, submissive, Scripture-filled, and industrious.

5. MARY COULD KEEP A SECRET

But more, we should honor Mary because of her willingness to ponder all the things God was doing. Mary had the ability to keep things to herself, a talent rarely found today. A. T. Robertson shares some interesting insights.

> Could Mary tell her mother the words of the angel? Was her mother living? We are told nothing, though one infers that both father and mother are dead. We do not know the names of her father and mother, though legend gives them as Joachim of Nazareth and Anna of Bethlehem. It is probable that Mary belonged to the tribe of Judah and the lineage of David as Joseph did (Luke 1:32, 69; 2:[4]). The Syriac Sinaitic manuscript for Luke 2:[4] has, "because they were both of the house of David." Mary was a kinswoman of Elisabeth (Luke 1:36) who belonged to the tribe of Levi, but that fact does not prove that Mary herself was of the tribe of Levi, for intermarriage between the tribes did occur. The family of Mary was probably a humble one as she was betrothed to Joseph the carpenter. That does not mean poverty, for the one or at least the chief carpenter of the town would naturally be a man of solid and substantial standing. Mary was already living at Nazareth when the angel Gabriel appeared to her.
>
> Mary could not and did not speak to Joseph about her wonderful secret. It was too sudden and too soon. There was only one

person in the world to whom she could go, and she had to open her heart to someone. That person was Elisabeth down in the hill country of Judea. To her she quickly made her way and found a surprising welcome, for Elizabeth knew at once that Mary was the woman of God's choice and sang her hymn of praise to Mary (Luke 1:42-45).[1]

Luke tells us that Mary pondered or, literally, considered all the things that were happening to her. She kept them in her heart (Luke 2:19).

After the angelic announcement, she pondered the message of the angel. After meeting Elisabeth, she pondered all the implications of being selected as God's chosen instrument. When the shepherds came to visit the Christ Child, she pondered the wonder of it all.

She didn't boast to the neighbors or share the news throughout the community. She pondered all these things in her heart. This pondering displays a devout, modest, worshipful, believing woman!

Mary believed in Jesus because she had pondered much about Jesus. She watched Him grow and mature. She knew that He was no ordinary son. She observed Him develop into manhood and begin His earthly ministry, and she pondered all that God was doing.

Mary was there when the crowd called out, "Crucify him! Crucify him!" She watched the soldiers nail Him to the cross, yet she did not intercede for Him, for she knew His true purpose. Mary knew that Jesus was indeed the Son of God, the Redeemer of mankind, the Saviour of the world.

CONCLUSION

May God give us mothers today like Mary!

And yet, let us remember that Mary, too, was a person with needs. Mary was a woman worthy of recognition, yet she was

1. A. T. Robertson, *The Mother of Jesus, Her Problems and Her Glory* (New York: Doran, 1925), pp. 17-18.

also a woman in need of a Saviour. Mary will be in heaven not because Jesus was her child but because Jesus was her Saviour, Lord, and Redeemer.

We honor Mary for her purity, her submissive spirit, her knowledge of the Bible, her industry, and for her willingness to ponder all the things that God had done. May each mother seek these same qualities that Mary possessed so that we, too, can bring glory to His Son, Jesus Christ the Saviour!

NINE

WHAT'S HAPPENING TO THE FAMILY?

Introduction

What is happening to the family? Is marriage on the way out? These questions are being asked more and more as divorce rates soar and broken homes multiply. Although the American family today enjoys its highest standard of living ever, there are signs that the home is in critical condition. What are the reasons for this crisis? Several reasons have been suggested.

1. Broken families

First, the family is fragmented. In other words, it does not hold together any longer than circumstances compel it to.

Thirty years ago, Harvard's sociologist Pitirim Sorokin predicted, "Divorces and separations will increase until any profound difference between socially sanctioned marriages and illicit sex-relationship disappears. . . . The main sociocultural functions of the family will further decrease until the family becomes a mere incidental cohabitation of male and female, while the home will be an overnight parking place."[1] What a horrible prediction. While this gloomy forecast has not yet been realized, there are many signs that indicate Dr. Sorokin's prediction contains much truth.

Shocking predictions are being voiced today by professional people throughout the world concerning the very institution of marriage. The *London Observer* printed a headline some time ago that asked, "Are we the last married generation?" A member of England's Official Marriage Guidance Council has predicted that engagements and weddings will soon be something of the past.

In a *Newsweek* cover story, general editor Richard Boeth sug-

1. Pitirim Sorokin, "Marriage," *Ladies Home Journal* 8 (September 1971):192.

gested that it is futile to believe there can be any reversal of this trend. "It is novel and bizarre of us latter-day Westernoids to imagine that we can make something tolerable of marriage. It doesn't seem to have occurred to any earlier era that this was even possible. The Greeks railed against marriage [while] the Romans mocked and perverted it."[2]

It is no secret that mankind has, throughout the centuries, perverted God's plan for family living. But despite the past record of sinful man, statistics tell us that today's marriage picture is the darkest ever. Divorce is bulldozing our society to ruin. In 1912, the census revealed that one in every twelve marriages ended in divorce. In 1932, one in every six marriages failed. Today there are two divorces for every three marriages performed.

Professional psychologist Dr. Lacey Hall says, "The Christian needs to realize what is happening to the family if he is to understand the forces shaping his own home, his own children, the families in his church and the homes in his neighborhood."[3]

2. ROOTLESS FAMILIES

A second reason for this crisis of the family is that the average family is rootless. Since the end of World War II, America has been on the move. Twenty percent of the population change their place of residence annually. Industry is demanding people who *will* move. One-third of all families with husbands under thirty-five years of age move each year.

In an article in *Moody Monthly,* Dr. Lacey Hall suggests that this mobility is changing the roots of the home.

> When the family moves, it has to adjust to new housing, new schools, and new friends. . . . And this often leads to insecurity and instability.
>
> A recent best-seller on the white collar class compares these conditions to the nursery that advertised, "We move our trees every

2. Richard Boeth, "Connubial Blitz: It Was Ever Thus," *Newsweek* 81 (March 12, 1973):56.
3. Lacey Hall, "What's Happening to the American Family?" *Moody Monthly* 67 (July-August 1967):26-28.

year so they won't grow deep roots." In other words, the nursery deliberately kept the root systems on its trees shallow so they could be transplanted easily. But they did not warn that such trees, without deep top roots, would not withstand the storms.[4]

And many of our families today are facing this same danger.

3. LONELY FAMILIES

Third, there is a lack of communication between family members today. The result of this development is a loss of oneness and togetherness. In many homes the husband, wife, and children all come and go as they please, often failing even to check in. Even though together, they are virtually alone. In an atmosphere such as this, real communication is impossible, and the family structure breaks down.

Yes, the family is in trouble. And let us remember that although the Christian home should be different, it is not exempt from these same problems.

Some time ago a mother shared with me concerning her married son who had just committed suicide. "Apples do not fall far from the trees," she said, as she spoke of the problems her son had experienced. She told me how her boy had capped a whirlwind romance by entering a hasty marriage. His wife had really never gotten to know him. All his weaknesses were brushed over until after the honeymoon.

Soon his wife discovered that he was a heavy drinker, emotionally immature, and totally lacking in responsibility. He was no more reliable than a cracked barometer. He was a poor marriage risk. Shortly after the birth of their first child, he deserted the family, and the marriage ended in divorce. Five years later he was dead, a victim of his own hand.

"He was just like his father," said the mother. "All of his faults he learned from my husband. Apples do not fall far from the trees."

Throughout the Scriptures, we are told that we reap exactly

4. Ibid.

what we sow. "Be sure your sin will find you out" (Num 32: 23).

4. SINFUL FAMILIES

The book of Exodus tells us about the children of Israel as they traveled through the wilderness. There, as they pitched their tents around Mount Sinai, God gave them His immutable Law. In explaining the first commandment, Exodus 20:5 states, "I the LORD thy God am a jealous God, visiting the iniquity of the fathers upon the children unto the third and fourth generation of them that hate me."

This verse is speaking about the sins of the parents. Moses was so impressed by this statement that he repeated it again in Exodus 34:7. And years later, when the children of Israel wavered between fervor and fear, Moses recalled these exact words in Deuteronomy 5:9. They were unforgettable to him. He saw God write them upon the tables of stone, and they were written upon the tablet of his mind. These words were terrifying then, and they are terrifying now. Our children reap the result of our sins to the third and fourth generation.

Every second, a baby is born somewhere in our world. For the most part, aside from the fact that we all are born with sinful natures, those children are emotionally, physically, and morally capable of developing into happy, adjusted adults. Yet many grow up to be just the opposite: miserable, unhappy, and frustrated. Why? Largely because of the sins of their parents.

In a study of the broken home, *Newsweek* magazine quoted one wife and mother who realized the effect her divorce had upon her eldest son: "We are very concerned with him," said the mother. "Lance has suffered psychic damage from all of this. . . . I laugh at a lot of things Lance does when I really should cry."[5] That boy suffered as a result of his parents' sin.

A Chinese proverb states, "In a broken nest there are few whole eggs." Sad to say, today there are literally thousands of

5. Boeth, p. 49.

emotionally disturbed children, products of shattered marriages. It behooves every parent to do everything possible to avoid a broken home.

Out of one thousand girls in an eastern Pennsylvania reform school, only eighty-seven came from homes in which there was a normal husband-wife relationship. More than nine hundred were from broken homes.

The late J. Edgar Hoover attributed our exploding crime rate to the sins of the parents. He felt that scandal in our nation is frequently due to broken homes, an attitude that God is not necessary in our way of life, and the idea that morality is old-fashioned.

It is not surprising to me that our nation's crime rate continues to climb. We have become a secularized society. We are living in an age when children are told God is dead, the church is irrelevant, and the former moral codes are outdated. We live in a world that is saturated by sex and given over to greed. The apostle Paul wrote to the church at Galatia, "Be not deceived; God is not mocked: for whatsoever a man soweth, that shall he also reap. For he that soweth to his flesh shall of the flesh reap corruption; but he that soweth to the Spirit shall of the Spirit reap life everlasting" (Gal 6:7-8).

"Apples do not fall far from the trees."

Lord Byron, the poet, was handsome, witty, and gifted, yet his life was a tragedy. At age thirty-six he wrote:

> The flower and fruit of love are gone.
> I've nothing left but the worm, the canker, and the grief.
> Neither glacier, mountain, torrent, forest or cloud
> > can lighten the weight upon my heart,
> > or enable me to lose my wretched identity.

Byron's ancestors, as far back as they can be traced, were violent, passionate, and unrestrained in morals. Byron lived as his parents lived. He openly violated all standards of morality and righteousness. He, indeed, bore the sins of his parents. Although he left imperishable poetry, Lord Byron also left an imperishable example of what happens to children who are neglected by careless parents.

5. SUCCESSFUL FAMILIES

There is no secret of a happy home. There is no magic formula to follow. But God's Word is perfectly clear when it instructs parents to bring up their children in "the nurture and admonition of the Lord" (Eph 6:4).

A. SUCCESSFUL FAMILIES ARE BUILT ON THE WORD OF GOD

God instructed the Israelites to devote themselves to the Scriptures and to teach and instruct their children in the precepts of Jehovah. "And thou shalt teach them diligently unto thy children, and shalt talk of them when thou sittest in thine house, and when thou walkest by the way, and when thou liest down, and when thou risest up" (Deut 6:7).

This is the way it should be in every family. The careful reading of the Word of God and family prayer are essentials in building a successful family.

B. SUCCESSFUL FAMILIES RESULT FROM GODLY PARENTS

The Bible says, "Train up a child in the way he should go: and when he is old, he will not depart from it" (Prov 22:6).

The Old Testament tells us about Absalom, the third son of David. This young man had every opportunity to be something, but he was petted and fondled by overindulgent parents. He became thoughtless and reckless. Law meant nothing to him. Self-gratification was the rule of his life.

On one occasion, Absalom decided to kill his half brother for ravishing his sister. Then he conspired to overthrow his father, David. As David's soldiers went out after him, David called, "Deal gently for my sake with the young man" (2 Sam 18:5).

Absalom followed in the footsteps of his father; he was a victim of the sins of his parents.

It is a colossal sin to neglect one's family. A man's wife and children should not be forced to compete with the newspaper or television for attention. Rather, a father should give himself to the members of his family.

"And, ye fathers," writes Paul, "bring them up in the nurture and admonition of the Lord" (Eph 6:4). To bring into this world an immortal soul is probably the greatest responsibility of life. The Christian father must be an example to his family. He must be what he expects his children to become.

Two boys were compelled by their father to go to church. When they became teenagers, they stopped. The father sternly reprimanded his sons and asked the reason. The older boy said, "Dad, we figure that if church isn't good enough for you, it isn't good enough for us."

All of us are examples for good or evil. Each one of us is a blueprint by which children build their lives.

C. Successful families are church related

The Church is important because it is the organization of God, built upon the foundation of Jesus Christ. And it will never pass away. Someone has said, "Though the church has many critics, it has no rivals." Despite the turmoil and tribulation it may go through, despite the neglect it may receive, the Church will remain. It will survive every onslaught and every attack, because it is God's institution.

Once a person has received Jesus Christ as Saviour, he needs to be built up in the faith. He needs to receive spiritual instruction and to share with other believers. He needs to have opportunity for Christian fellowship. The Church, through its ministries, is an instrument of training and provides an atmosphere for spiritual growth.

I cannot overemphasize the importance of the local church in the formation of solid, spiritual, successful families. The familiar saying is true, "Families that pray together stay together." If you have church in the home, you will always have your home in church.

CONCLUSION

What is your family like? Is it anchored to the rock of God's Word, or is it drifting on the sea of uncertainty? Are you as a parent setting an example for your children to follow? Are you teaching them the Scriptures? Are you leading them into spiritual maturity? Have you guided them into a church that will encourage them in the things of God?

"Be not deceived; God is not mocked: for whatsoever a man soweth, that shall he also reap" (Gal 6:7).

TEN

THREE GREAT
MEMORIALS

INTRODUCTION

What does Memorial Day mean to you? For some, it's just a holiday approaching summer, a day away from work, when budding trees and shrubs assure us that the time for outdoor enjoyment is but a breath away.

For others, Memorial Day brings memories from the past: flags, parades, flowers for a grave of some loved one who once marched off to war.

Each year during the month of March, a small group of people meets in a Chicago park. They gather to honor Clarence Darrow, the famous criminal lawyer, Braving the cold March winds, and often snow and sleet, the group conducts a brief memorial service at the bridge from which the lawyer's ashes were scattered in 1938.

That is a memorial for one man—the man who, fifty years ago, faced the famous orator William Jennings Bryan in the historic evolution trial at Dayton, Tennessee. But this Memorial Day, an entire nation will honor more than one million Americans who gave their lives in wartime for our country.

Decoration Day, as many call it, has been observed for more than a hundred years. It was first officially proclaimed in 1868, shortly after the War Between the States.

Is Memorial Day still meaningful? Or is it just another holiday? There was a day in the memory of many when each town and city turned out in full force. Men for whom military life was but a memory struggled into too-tight uniforms to march down Main Street to the cemetery. Drill squads fired salutes, and citizens returned to their homes with the notes of taps still echoing in their minds and memories. And that was good, for we need a time to pause and look back on the way we have come. We need to remember that, with all our imperfections, America is a great place to live and rear a family. It is a place of many freedoms, a nation where, in the long run, people outweigh their government.

What America is and offers has not just happened. God has moved mightily in our two hundred years of history. With Kipling we say:

> Lord God of Hosts, be with us yet,
> Lest we forget—lest we forget!

What is a memorial? The dictionary says it is something which serves to preserve remembrance, which brings to mind. It is something which helps us to remember.

A memorial can be a special day, a bridge, a building, or a musical composition. The list is almost endless. Such memorials focus on men and women from the human viewpoint. But there are also memorials which point us to the work and will of God.

One is the rainbow. Have you ever thought of the rainbow as a memorial? Genesis 9 tells us that it is God's memorial, assuring us that He will never again judge the earth by flood.

Then, too, Jacob set up a memorial at Bethel. It was the stone on which he had pillowed his head before his dream of the ladder reaching down from heaven. Through the rest of his life, it was his reminder that God had appeared and spoken to him.

Jewish men wore memorials on their garments. They were tassels with cords of blue. God commanded they wear the tassels to remind them of His commandments.

When God parted the Jordan River to let Israel cross over to the promised land, He told each tribe to carry a stone out of the riverbed. That pile of stones on the riverbank became a memorial of His great miracle in their behalf.

These were memory aids, reminders to the Jewish people that they belonged to God, that He had done great things for them, and that He had a great purpose for their lives. But God also has memorials for the whole human race. I have mentioned one, the rainbow. But there are others.

1. THE WEEKLY DAY OF REST

The Bible tells us that God created the earth in six successive days and that He rested on the seventh. In Genesis 2, we read, "And God blessed the seventh day, and sanctified it: because that in it he had rested from all his work" (v. 3).

This became the pattern for men: six days for work, one day for rest. Much later it became an important part of God's covenant with the Jews. It was also included in the Ten Commandments.

Every day of rest should be a memorial of God's creation. We should never forget, as Psalm 100 says, "It is he that hath made us, and not we ourselves; we are his people, and the sheep of his pasture" (v. 3).

The Bible tells us that our memorial day of rest also speaks of Christ's saving work on our behalf and the rest He has in heaven for those who trust in Him.

One of the great hymns of John Newton voices this important truth:

> Safely through another week
> God has brought us on our way.

A later line goes on to say,

> Day of all the week the best,
> Emblem of eternal rest.

Since apostolic times, New Testament Christians have worshiped on the first day of the week, the day on which Christ rose from the dead. Thus our Lord's Day is also a great memorial of Christ's resurrection.

I wonder, my friend, are you keeping God's memorial day of Christ's resurrection? What a meaningful memorial day it really is!

2. THE FEAST OF PASSOVER

The feast of the Passover is a special observance which has been celebrated for centuries by the Jews during the first month of the Jewish year. It recalls a wonderful but terrible night in Egypt—the night when God delivered His people from four hundred years of harsh slavery.

The Passover was God's provision for Israel's safety during the last of ten great plagues which God had brought upon Egypt. In a final, climactic blow, the God of life and death brought death to the eldest son of each family in the land. Even first-born animals died. But He spared the Jews on a very special basis.

You remember what He did. The Jews were told to kill a lamb and to place a splash of blood above and at either side of the door. You can read the record in Exodus 12: "And when I see the blood, I will pass over you, and the plague shall not be upon you to destroy you" (v. 13).

Do you get the picture? No one was to leave his blood-marked house. God simply said, "This is what I'm going to do. This is how you can be safe." And God did what He had promised. Death came that night to Egypt, from Pharaoh's palace to the humblest beggar's hovel. The Bible says, "There was a great cry in Egypt; for there was not a house where there was not one dead" (Exod 12:30).

Because of that unforgettable night, the Passover feast was a great memorial for every Jew. But it also looked ahead. In the fullness of time, there would come a day when God would say to the peoples of the world, "Here is My Passover Lamb, My only Son. I've sent Him to earth to die on a cross for you. Put His blood on the door of your life, and I will spare you for His sake."

Think about this for a moment. Suppose there had been Jews in Egypt that first Passover night who failed to get the point? Suppose they had said, "This doesn't make much sense to me. I don't need a lamb. I'll mark my house some other way." If some had done this, what would have happened in their homes?

The picture is too plain to miss. God has extended His Passover to all the world, because He loves the world. I wonder, have you marked the doorway of your life with the blood of Jesus Christ?

The feast of Passover was for God's chosen people, but it is rich with meaning for us all. Have you let its memorial message speak to you?

First we noticed God's day of rest, and then, His Passover. But there is a third memorial of God's love that we must also note. Though linked with the Passover feast, it is quite different from it.

3. THE LORD'S SUPPER

The Lord's Supper is the one memorial our Lord Himself commanded. Jesus and His disciples were in an upper room on the night of His betrayal. They were seated for the Passover meal. As they sat together at the table, Jesus passed a broken loaf of bread and a cup to each in turn.

These, He said, were to remind them of His body that would be broken and His blood that would be poured out so the gift of salvation could be free to all. "Do this," He said, "in remembrance of me." "When you do it," He added, "you will picture my death for sinners till I come again" (1 Cor 11:25-26, author's paraphrase).

Communion is God's great memorial of love for us. It reminds us that He gave Himself for us as individuals. Just as each Christian must partake of the bread and the cup individually, so he must personally receive Christ's forgiveness and new life.

The Lord's Supper is also the memorial of Christ, the person who loves us. "Do this," He said, "in remembrance of me." Communion should remind us not merely of Christ's work for us, but of our Saviour and Lord whom we will someday see.

93

ELEVEN

A TIME
TO REMEMBER

Memorial Day reminds us of the importance of "remembering."

Locked away, down deep inside your heart, is a treasure house that only you can open. Inside are memories and visions from the past that time can never erase.

Not all of these memories are pleasant. There are some sad recollections. Some memories are even tinged with tears. But there are happy memories, too, recollections you would not exchange for any sum of money in the world.

Memory! What a wonderful gift! Our memories neatly store away many good things from the past. Memory also helps to carry us through the present. Without the power to remember, we would stumble through a world of terror and confusion, unable to profit from anything we had learned before. We wouldn't even know that we could quench our thirst at a drinking fountain, or that a red traffic light means "stop," or that a mailbox is a place to mail a letter.

Memory is a strange and mysterious gift. Psychologists tell us that it is not really a storehouse or a file which we fill and empty at will. Rather, it is a process by which we rehearse past experiences and call up old associations. And yet, we do forget! Even important things gradually fade away. That's one reason why we have days set aside like Memorial Day. They are memory aids. Even with their help, we find ourselves forgetting things we had hoped we would remember.

Perhaps already at your house someone has been hard pressed to answer a childish question, "What is Memorial Day?" or, "Why do we have Decoration Day?"

Decoration Day emerged from the shadows of the War Between the States. It was first observed in the South. Before the close of the war, a group of women decorated the graves of those who had died in that war. A few years later, in 1868, May 30 was set aside as a day for placing flowers on the graves of soldiers throughout the United States of America. They decorated the graves.

Soon Decoration Day was observed each year across the country. Since World War I, this day in May has been used to honor the fallen dead of all our wars. We ought to honor these heroes of the past. We should remember the price they have paid for all that we enjoy today. Parents, perhaps this Memorial Day you should take your children to some cemetery. Be sure they understand that others gave their lives in sacrifice. This great heritage of ours has cost far more than they will understand.

How quickly we forget. We forget how much we owe to our country. But even more tragic, we forget how much we owe to our God. Each Lord's Day should really be a memorial day, to remind us of God's mercies. A forgetful heart soon becomes a foolish heart. An ungrateful attitude soon becomes a highway to ungodly living.

The person or nation that forgets God is as foolish and trouble-bound as the one who forgets that a red light means "stop" or that he can quench his thirst at a drinking fountain.

As we consider Memorial Day, let me remind you of four mighty truths our nation should remember.

1. REMEMBER THE GREATNESS AND GLORY OF GOD

We should remember the greatness and glory of God. First John 1 tells us that "God is light, and in him is no darkness at all" (v. 5). What is John saying? Simply that the man or woman who knows God and looks to Him will never be disappointed with God's character nor ever find Him limited. He is all light and no darkness.

You see, God is holy. This means, among other things, that His character and personality are in perfect balance. You and I may have too much temper or too little courage, or we may be too strict or too indulgent. Not so with God. He is just, yet He is gracious. He is patient, and yet exacting. He is impartial, but loving.

Oh, yes, you can make up your own concept of God, and many people do. They see Him as a God who can be fooled or deceived, a God who can be pushed around, persuaded, or put off. Others imagine Him as a God who created the world but has let it get completely out of hand. Some have even imagined a God who is no longer living.

But such concepts do not change God as He really is. He is the unchanging God, and we will one day meet Him as He really is, regardless of our concept.

For centuries God has permitted men to make their idols. Some idols are of wood or stone, while some are intellectual concepts. But God Himself remains the same. Every person will one day stand before Him as He is, not as he has imagined Him to be. What is God really like? The only way to know is through written revelation, the Bible.

We have heard much of a generation gap, a credibility gap, and other kinds of gaps. But I would remind you of a Creator gap. There is an infinite gap between man and his Creator because of sin. We were made in His image and likeness, that's true, but we are creatures subject to limitations of time and space. He is the great Creator, the Giver of life. He is infinite and eternal.

The point is that if you know God as He is, you will be compelled to reverence and honor Him, to set Him above all others and all else. That, in essence, is what the apostle Peter is saying in 1 Peter 3:15, "But sanctify [or set apart] the Lord God in your hearts."

God is to be set apart in our love, set apart in our lives, set apart in our thinking. He is to be revered, served, depended on and trusted in, obeyed, and made the rejoicing of our hearts. He should be the joy and the center of our lives.

Yes, we need to remember the greatness and glory of our God.

2. REMEMBER THE RIGHTS OF GOD

We also should remember the rights of God.

Ours is a day when many voices are raised in defense of human rights—the rights of those accused of criminal acts, the rights of men and women to use or misuse their bodies as they wish, the rights of individuals to pollute the public mind in order to make money.

We hear about the right of women to cut off the lives of infants they have helped conceive. We hear about the rights of those who deny the existence of the God who gives them breath.

But what about God's rights? What about His first rights as Creator, His rights as our Redeemer? Does He have a prior claim to obedience, to trust, and to worship?

You men who are mechanics, what would you do with a machine which could not be controlled? What would you cooks do with a dessert that quickly spoiled or that no one could enjoy?

Does not God have rights over His creation? Yet, by and large, men and women ignore these rights, neglect His Word, and choose their own prerogatives.

Revelation 4:11 reveals a scene in heaven. The elders around the throne of God are saying, "Thou art worthy, O Lord, to receive glory and honour and power: for thou hast created all things, and for thy pleasure they are and were created."

Today we hear about "the forgotten man." But the forgotten One of our day and generation is Almighty God.

Yes, we need a memorial day for remembering the greatness and the glory of God and for remembering the rights of our great God.

3. REMEMBER THE JUDGMENTS OF GOD

Judgments is an unpopular word today. It speaks of getting things right, of correction and punishment.

Does God really punish sin? Yes, He does! The entire Bible, from Genesis to Revelation, tells us that God is mighty in His judgments.

The ungodly seem to think otherwise. As the psalmist says of the wicked man in Psalm 10, verse 5, "Thy judgments are far above out of his sight."

Another passage, 1 Timothy 5:24, reminds us. "Some men's sins are open beforehand, going before to judgment; and some men they follow after." In other words, some sins bring immediate and open judgment, and, in other cases, judgment waits until after death. The apostle Paul speaks of this second kind of judgment in Romans 2:5 and 6: "But after thy hardness and impenitent heart treasurest up unto thyself wrath against the day of wrath and revelation of the righteous judgment of God; who will render to every man according to his deeds."

Does God let man get by with sin? Think of the terrible and far-reaching judgment when man sinned in Eden. The whole human race is still under that judgment.

Think of the judgment of the Flood. God waited in patience while the ark was being built. Each day brought opportunity for repentance. But the day came when God closed the door. Opportunities were past. The floods came, and a whole world perished.

And what of the nation Israel? For centuries God pleaded with them to turn from idolatry and other sins. When they kept saying no, He brought their nation down to dust.

Oh, my friends, God so hates sin that He poured out wrath and judgment on His Son. Never forget, the cross of Jesus Christ is final proof that God is a God of holiness and justice.

Revelation, chapter 6, speaks of a coming day when kings and the great and the rich and the mighty and the slaves and the free will hide themselves in caves, calling to the mountains and rocks, "Fall on us, and hide us from the face of him that sitteth on the throne, and from the wrath of the Lamb: for the great day of his wrath is come; and who shall be able to stand?" (Rev 6:16-17).

Yes, we need to remember these solemn things: the greatness and glory of God, the sovereign rights of God, the great judgments of God. But we need to remember one thing more.

4. REMEMBER THE LOVE AND GRACE OF GOD

God is holy, but He reaches down to us in pure love and grace. As Psalm 103 reminds us, "He hath not dealt with us after our sins, nor rewarded us according to our iniquities" (v. 10).

Isaiah, chapter 1, pleads, "Though your sins be as scarlet, they shall be as white as snow; though they be red like crimson, they shall be as wool" (v. 18).

The great good news of the Gospel is that God became flesh in the person of Jesus Christ. He bore our sins on the cross. He suffered and died and was buried and raised again, that we might have forgiveness.

CONCLUSION

My friend, is Jesus Christ your personal Saviour? Are you trusting and serving Him? You cannot receive His gift of forgiveness and everlasting life unless you receive Him as your own Saviour.

There are so many who have never settled their account with God. There are so many who do not have assurance of salvation. Yet God wants you to be sure. There are so many who have given their life to Christ, but who have tried to take it back again. They want it for themselves.

Life is not just food and drink. It is not merely a job and a car and a vacation once or twice a year. It is not even the "good things" of life. Before this time next year, thousands of us alive now will have passed from this life forever. Make this a real Memorial Day, a day of remembering. Remember God's greatness, His rights, His judgments, and His marvelous grace, and live by faith in Christ with eternity in view.

TWELVE

WHICH WAY, AMERICA?

INTRODUCTION

The United States of America is actually a very young nation. In fact, our entire two hundred years of history have been spanned by the lives of just four presidents. When Thomas Jefferson died, Abraham Lincoln was a young man of seventeen. Lincoln's life was short, but when he died, Woodrow Wilson was a boy of eight. By the time the nation mourned for President Wilson, Gerald Ford had reached the age of ten.

Yes, the United States has risen rapidly. But could our fall be just as quick? Let's look the future full in the face and ask, "Which way, America?"

Beginning September 1, 1976, a ban on fireworks went into effect across the United States. From now on, July 4 should be a great deal quieter than ever before. Actually, fireworks, for safety reasons, have been in full retreat for many years. But another kind of quietness is far less reassuring. For many people, there is a lack of enthusiasm in celebrating our birthday. The big bang has been quite subdued. Some have little taste for a lighthearted celebration. In fact, instead of a birthday party atmosphere, there's a serious mood across the nation.

This is the feeling coming from many directions. *Time* magazine said, "The belief that America . . . has created a kind of heaven on earth, has been badly damaged."[1] People are disillusioned and confused about their lives and the future of this country. A recent Harris survey placed Congress at the bottom of the list of United States institutions in which the public has

1. Henry Grunwald, "The Morning After the Fourth: Have We Kept Our Promise?" *Time* 106 (July 14, 1975):19.

some degree of confidence. Only 9 percent of the American people express a great deal of confidence in our congressmen. The executive branch rates only slightly higher with a confidence rating of 11 percent.

Public confidence in nongovernmental groups and individuals is little better. Only 16 percent show confidence in people running major businesses. Only 24 percent have confidence in those leading organized religion. Twenty-three percent have confidence in military leaders, and only 20 percent have confidence in the nation's press. Voters are disappointed and apathetic. We are not experiencing a material crisis, despite high prices and joblessness, but a spiritual and psychological depression. People are not happy. Many ordinary people have felt these things for some time. The United States, in spite of our incredible past, is facing some serious problems.

As Archibald MacLeish has said, the founding of America was more than a political event. It was a promise, a promise to the colonists and to the world at large, that people could govern themselves, that they could live in freedom and equality. The assumption was that they would act in accord with reason and with equity, and out of this came what we often call "the American dream."

This was the hope and dream that we and our children could reach a level of well-being and opportunity such as other nations have never known. But now many people wonder whether or not our American dream has vanished, not so much because of enemies without but because of our weaknesses within.

What is this condition which many sense as very real, yet still undefined and still untreated? Before trying to answer, let me mention some of the more obvious symptoms of our national condition.

The first is *disillusionment and cynicism.* Some have lost their enthusiasm and optimism about the future. There is a lack of old-fashioned trust and confidence in one another.

The second is a *loss of national integrity and character.* Everyone knows crime is increasing. Violence throws a shadow over the security of our citizens. Stealing is epidemic. Divorce is shattering marriages at an astounding rate.

The third is *preoccupation with unworthy things* such as materialism, sex, pleasure, satisfaction here and now without regard for others. We have lost much of the will to sacrifice for the good of others and for the national good.

The fourth is—and I am persuaded that this is basic—we have *lost our fear of God* and our awareness of His sovereignty.

As a nation, how far can we go before we reach the point of no return? Some believe we have already passed that point, and that even now we lack the will and the determination to change. No nation has ever known just when it has arrived at that place until it was too late!

When I speak of turning back, I do not mean mere reform or self-correction. I personally believe that it is too late for that. I am talking about a sincere turning back to God for divine help and intervention.

Can a nation cry out to God for help when the essence of its problem lies in its lack of will to follow God? The answer is yes. God hears the weakest cry, and He responds to need. Listen to the cry of the prophet Jeremiah in Lamentations 5:21: "Turn thou us unto thee, O LORD, and we shall be turned; renew our days as of old."

This is America's need as she celebrates her birthday!

This same prayer is found in Psalm 80. Fervently and earnestly, the psalmist prays, "Turn us again, O God, and cause thy face to shine; and we shall be saved" (v. 3). This Old Testament verse tells us three vital things.

1. WE NEED TO BE TURNED

We need to be turned; we need God's help. We cannot turn ourselves by laws or legislation or education or by any kind of rational choice. Our beloved America needs a change of heart.

Our problems are the problems of the inner life of sinful wills and sinful ways.

The bitter truth is that though America once knew God, at least to fear Him, in two hundred years we have largely turned away. This is not to say that ours has ever been a wholly Christian nation. But we have known the moral and spiritual strength that comes from the fear of God, awareness of the Bible, and overruling faith in Jesus Christ.

In two hundred years we have moved a long way toward pride and trust in men. We have not feared to push aside the Word of God. We have magnified the rights of men and minimized the rights of God. Worst of all, we have heard the Gospel of Jesus Christ, but as a nation we have esteemed it lightly.

Romans 1:18 states, "For the wrath of God is revealed from heaven against all ungodliness and unrighteousness of men, who hold the truth in unrighteousness." America's deepest sin is its lack of esteem for the Word of God. Although we have known the Gospel, we have held the truth carelessly, and now the night is closing in.

Not only does America need to be turned.

2. We need God's turning

We need God's turning. Psalm 80 says, "Turn us again, O God of hosts" (v. 7). Only God can meet our need. He is the God of the hosts of heaven, and yet He knows the human heart.

And only God can change the heart. Knowledge cannot do it. Experience will not do it. Law cannot do it. We can try to profit from past mistakes. We can even make good resolutions. We can bind ourselves with restraints. But without the mighty Gospel of the cross, nothing will save us.

There is really only one doorway to eternal life. That door is Jesus Christ. Jesus said in John 10:9, "I am the door: by me if any man enter in, he shall be saved."

Jesus Christ did not die for nations but for people, who constitute the nations. No nation can rise above the faith and character of its individual citizens.

America has a choice to make! Either we must turn back to God by faith in Jesus Christ, or we will join the fate of other long-forgotten nations.

The Word of God warns plainly in Psalm 9:17, "The wicked shall be turned into hell, and all the nations that forget God." Let me repeat, "All the nations that forget God."

But there is hope. The prayer of Psalm 80 promises that if a nation cries out to God, we shall be saved.

3. WE SHALL BE SAVED

Yes, God can meet our nation's need. If we sincerely call out to God to "turn us again" and cause His face to shine upon us, "we shall be saved." That was the experience of Israel. Seven times in the period recorded in the book of Judges, Israel fell away from God. Seven times she knew the bitterness of bondage. Seven times, in tears, Israel turned to God. And God delivered her every time.

Yes, God responds to nations. Hear what He says in Jeremiah 18:8: "If that nation, against whom I have pronounced, turn from their evil, I will repent of the evil that I thought to do unto them." Much more is involved than just a withholding of judgment. Jeremiah 24:7 says, "And I will give them an heart to know me, that I am the LORD: and they shall be my people, and I will be their God: for they shall return unto me with their whole heart." My friend, this is what America needs: a change of heart. And only God can give that.

Historian Arnold Toynbee pointed out that nineteen major civilizations have existed since the beginning of time. Only five remain today, of which our Western civilization is one.

But you say, "We cannot turn the tide of unbelief." No, but God can ! I think of Nineveh, the capital of the great Assyrian Empire. Like modern New York, it was a complex of cities with walls nearly eight miles in circumference. Who doesn't know the story of Jonah, the reluctant prophet, who sailed the other way and refused to go preach repentance to that great city? We know all about the great fish which swallowed Jonah, only to cast him upon the shore.

But what happened next? It was to Nineveh that God sent Jonah when he was finally ready to obey. His message from God was plain and to the point. "Yet forty days, and Nineveh shall be overthrown" (3:4). The Bible tells us the whole city repented, from the greatest to the least. And God, in grace and mercy, spared the city for more than another century.

CONCLUSION

We do not need a prophet like Jonah. We have had hundreds of godly prophets. We have had the open Word of God. But we need to hear God's voice and turn to Him before it is too late. The future of our beloved United States of America may lie in the hands of our present generation. Before the next generation takes its place, America may be past the point of no return. How will you cast your vote?

Can we be trusted with the future of "the American dream"? Even more important, do American Christians have the vision and the faith to intercede and urge our nation to turn back to her rightful God and Sovereign? May we pray with the psalmist, "Turn us again, O God, and cause thy face to shine; and we shall be saved" (Psalm 80:3).

The Saviour is waiting. When the prodigal son, in the gospel of Luke, started for home, the father *ran* to meet him. If we individually turn in repentance, God's blessing *will* be upon us "and we shall be saved." As one person, will you make your decision to obey God's will? And as thousands of individuals turn to Jesus Christ, America will turn.

THIRTEEN

THE LABORER

INTRODUCTION

Each year, on the first Monday in September, America celebrates Labor Day. It's a day of parades, picnics, and political speeches. It is a time when we pay special recognition to the millions of Americans who are a part of this nation's mighty working force.

Edwin Markham, in his poem "The Man with the Hoe," paints a picture of the laborer.

> Bowed by the weight of centuries he leans
> Upon his hoe and gazes on the ground,
> The emptiness of ages in his face,
> And on his back the burden of the world.

1. WHY DO WE LABOR?

Throughout history, labor has been man's chief activity. Thomas Carlyle put it simply: "Labor is life."

According to Webster, labor always involves either physical or mental exertion. As a result of man's sin in the Garden of Eden, God told Adam that he would earn his bread by the sweat of his face (Gen 3:19). The ground would bring forth thorns and thistles, and man would be required to labor in the field. Gone were the ideal conditions of Eden. Instead of Adam's original occupation of "dressing" the garden, he and his descendants would now engage in burdensome toil.

This burdensome toil was and is the result of the curse God measured out in Genesis 3: "Cursed is the ground for thy sake; in sorrow shalt thou eat of it all the days of thy life" (v. 17). Sorrow is inevitable; it is a reality in each and every life. It is as inescapable as the toil in which each one must engage.

God told Adam that all his life would be filled with labor. He would toil until the day he returned to the dust of the earth from

111

which he was taken. It is interesting, yet ironic, to realize that that which we honor this week—labor—is a direct result of the judgment God passed upon man in the Garden of Eden. It is the result of sin!

The apostle Paul reminds us that all of creation groans under the blight of sin. In Romans 8:22, he writes, "For we know that the whole creation groaneth and travaileth in pain together until now." The Scripture plainly indicates that God intended for people to toil and work. The Bible sets forth the principle of labor.

Throughout the history of our country, the importance of labor has always been recognized. From its inception, this nation has been dedicated to the principle of hard work. As of Labor Day, 1976, the civilian labor force of the United States totaled close to 100 million persons. Each year our nation requires thousands of new engineers, nurses, mechanics, and sales personnel to fill the job openings developed by an expanding economy.

It is the labor of untold millions of men and women which has brought unequaled prosperity to this great land of ours. And only as we remember the value of true, hard work can we remain a strong and determined people.

Unfortunately, some people today have little respect for an honest day's work. There is a sign at the entrance of a great manufacturing plant that reads, "If you are like a wheelbarrow, going no farther than you are pushed, you need not apply for work here." Many people, it seems, need to be pushed in order to accomplish anything worthwhile.

Someone has said there are three kinds of people: those who make things happen; those who watch things happen; and those who have no idea what has happened. Today we need less watchers and more doers. It was the wise king Solomon who said, "Whatsoever thy hand findeth to do, do it with thy might" (Eccles 9:10). God's principle for man is work. God intended for us to work.

Labor Day is the day which is set aside to honor the millions of this nation's working men and women. In many cities and towns, there will be parades and special observances. But for most people, the day is dedicated to rest and recreation. It is an extra day of escape from the hectic work week.

To many, however, rest and relaxation will not come. For millions, the burdens of life will not be lifted simply because of another holiday. For despite the gigantic strides made by and for the working people of this country, despite the shorter work weeks and the greater salaries, men and women everywhere are burdened down with cares.

2. GOD'S CALL TO THE LABORER

It was to this kind of person that the invitation of Jesus was directed in Matthew 11: "Come unto me, all ye that labour and are heavy laden, and I will give you rest. Take my yoke upon you, and learn of me; for I am meek and lowly in heart: and ye shall find rest unto your souls. For my yoke is easy, and my burden is light" (vv. 28-30).

Who are the heavy ladened? On this occasion, Jesus was speaking of those who were not familiar with the grace of God. Isaiah referred to the people of his day as, "a people laden with iniquity" (Isa 1:4).

This Labor Day finds many people trapped in the web of sin and neglect of God.

Robert Burns, at a time when he was overcome by alcoholism, wrote, "O Life! thou art a galling load,/ Along a rough, a weary road,/ To wretches such as I." Robert Burns was obviously a man who was "heavy laden."

In his sarcastic description of life, William Shakespeare wrote, "Life's but a walking shadow, a poor player,/ That struts and frets his hour upon the stage,/ And then is heard no more; it is a tale/ Told by an idiot, full of sound and fury."

Atlas with the world on his shoulders had a light load compared to those away from God.

My friend, there are many today who "labor and are heavy laden." Many today are burdened by a lack of purpose. For them, life has no meaning and the future offers nothing but futility.

But, you ask, why is this so? Why are people heavy ladened and out of step with God? The answer is that God made man in *His* image, with rational and moral faculties. Man is a unique creation of God, different from all other creatures. And a man who fails to recognize God, a man who refuses to acknowledge God for who He is, cannot live with himself. Because of this, there can be no rest until we are reconciled or united with God through the person of Jesus Christ.

In the very beginning, God and man were friends. They walked and talked together. The Garden of Eden was a beautiful portrait of unity and friendship. Adam and God walked and talked together; they were partners.

But then rebellion entered the picture. Adam said, "I'll do things my way, I'll do what *I* want to do." As a result, men and women are weary, frustrated, and bored. They are "heavy laden" because of the rebellion and sin in their lives. Apart from Jesus Christ, life is a burden; it is a "galling load" filled with bitterness and disappointment.

3. THE GOSPEL AND THE DIGNITY OF LABOR

Labor Day is a special day on which we recognize the dignity of work and the rights of the worker. Jesus believed in the dignity of labor. He was concerned about the worker and his work. In Luke 10:7, he said, "The labourer is worthy of his hire."

Today, millions of people around the world belong to labor unions. Many of you reading this book are union members. Did you realize that the trade unions as we know them were originally an outgrowth of the spiritual revivals of John and Charles Wesley? In the early 1700s, working conditions in Britain were seemingly hopeless. Men worked sixteen or more hours a day six days a week. Little children as young as ten

114

years of age worked long hours deep in mines and in the factories. Women worked. Many died from accidents or simply from exhaustion. The working person, man, woman, or child, was little more than a slave to be exploited. Drunkenness, immorality, and hopelessness abounded.

History tells us that social liberty in England began as a result of a great return to God under the preaching of John Wesley. Men such as Bishop William Wilberforce and Lord Shaftesbury began to force legislation which brought relief to the working classes. Whenever and wherever the Gospel of Jesus Christ is truly preached, then as now, it results in earthly as well as heavenly changes.

4. LABOR AND THE WARNING OF GOD'S WORD

As we study the Word of God, we find that the Bible speaks to both the employer and the employee. Each has his responsibilities to fulfill. In James 5, wealthy employers are warned of God's judgment upon their evil deeds. They had spent their lives on earth having fun and satisfying their every whim at the expense of their employees. To these evil men, James declares, "Behold, the hire of the labourers who have reaped down your fields, which is of you kept back by fraud, crieth: and the cries of them which have reaped are entered into the ears of the Lord of sabaoth" (James 5:4).

James is simply saying that God hears the cry of the laborer who is cheated. God is aware of injustice, and He will be the final Judge.

In the book of Exodus, God's people Israel were being exploited by the Egyptians. In chapter 3, the Lord said, "I have surely seen the affliction of my people which are in Egypt, and have heard their cry by reason of their taskmasters; for I know their sorrows" (Exod 3:7). God sees, He hears, and He knows when a worker is treated unfairly. God cares about you, my friend.

At the same time, God also sees the laborer. The worker who

115

loafs on the job is guilty of stealing. The employee who pads his expense account or does outside business on company time, God sees. Failure to put in a good day's work is dishonest, and God knows.

No matter what your position this Labor Day weekend, Christ's invitation is still extended today. To employer and employee alike, Jesus says, "Come . . . and I will give you rest" (Matt 11:28). To the tired farmer coming from his fields, Jesus says, "Come." To the merchant with his wares, the fisherman with his nets, the laborer with his heavy load, to all these He says, "Come unto me . . . and I will give you rest." No matter how others have treated you, I will give you rest.

To those who labor, Jesus offers rest. Not simply physical comfort and refreshment, but eternal rest for their souls.

5. How to enter god's rest

As a young man, Augustine was literally exhausted from his pursuit of sinful lusts. After he had repented of his sin and turned to Jesus Christ, he said, "Our hearts were made for Thee, O Lord, and they are restless until they rest in Thee."

My friend, are you restless? Is there something missing in your life? Do you know anything about God's rest? Are you burdened down by a load of guilt and despair? Jesus offers the same invitation to you today that He offered two thousand years ago. "Come unto me, all ye that labour and are heavy laden, and I will give you rest." Won't you come to Him today? No matter who you are, no matter what you have done, Jesus waits to receive you today.

You can enter into God's rest by acknowledging your sinful condition and by acknowledging Jesus Christ as God's provision for your sin. Accept the rest that comes from being at one with God.

6. How to enjoy god's rest

Matthew 11:29 also states our future privilege and responsi-

116

bility: "Take my yoke upon you, and learn of me . . . and ye shall find rest unto your souls." After receiving the Saviour, as partners with God, we are to *take* and *learn*. "Take my yoke" and "learn of me."

Our Lord Jesus was always submissive to God the Father. He said, "I do always those things that please him" (John 8:29). My meat is to do the will of him that sent me, and to finish his work" (John 4:34).

Our yoke is to do the will of God. When we do this whole-heartedly, we find that His yoke is easy and His burden is light.

FOURTEEN

THANKFULNESS: THE ROAD BACK TO GOD

Three and a half centuries ago, a little band of men and women joined their hands and hearts in America's first Thanksgiving. With Indian guests, they gathered around a table for the New World's first Thanksgiving dinner. Measured by our standards, they did not have too much. Harvest was in, and they were grateful to God. But their needs were great, and there were no supermarkets down the street. Cold, hunger, and sickness threatened their very lives.

How far, in some ways, we have come since that first day of thanks in 1621. Today more than two hundred million people populate our land. We produce more food, more fuel, more finished products than any nation in the world. Measured by dollars and cents, our gross national product exceeds one trillion dollars and is climbing every year. Science and industry do our bidding. We can even send men to the moon.

But like the Pilgrims, we have great needs. We are concerned for energy and a growing number of critical materials. The richest nation in the world is perplexed and troubled by crucial shortages. Inflation is pushing up the cost of nearly everything the average family wants and needs. We have higher wages and more dollars, but they are buying less and less all the time. More serious still, our nation appears to stand at a crossroad of its history. The winds of moral and spiritual pollution threaten our future.

At such a time as this, real thankfulness may be just the turning point we need. For thankfulness to God can be a long and

119

important step back toward things we have forgotten. Why should we be thankful to God?

1. BECAUSE WE OWE IT TO HIM

In Revelation, chapters 4 and 5, we catch two glimpses of praise around the throne of heaven. In Revelation 4:11, we hear the song, "Thou art worthy, O Lord, to receive glory and honour and power: for thou hast created all things, and for thy pleasure they are and were created."

Have you ever considered this truth? God is worthy of our thanks because He is our Maker. "Know ye that the LORD he is God," says Psalm 100, "it is he that hath made us, and not we ourselves" (v. 3).

All that we are and have is from God's hand. The strength we have, the food and shelter that maintain our lives, the blood and breath within our bodies, the very time we have, here and in eternity to come, are a gift of our Creator. He is our Provider and Sustainer. Every necessity of life comes from His hand.

But God is more! In Revelation 5:12, we hear all heaven sing another song: "Worthy is the Lamb that was slain to receive power, and riches, and wisdom, and strength, and honor, and glory, and blessing." How thankful we should be that our Creator God is also our Redeemer. He was slain for our sins.

But there is another reason why we should give thanks to God.

2. BECAUSE TO ACKNOWLEDGE HIS GOODNESS IS TO SEE HIM AS HE IS

When you are thankful, you see God's love and goodness. Your eyes are wide open to His judgments. You are receptive to His will. Unthankfulness, by contrast, blinds the eyes. An unthankful person may not even know that God is in the picture.

An unthankful nation is no better. An unthankful nation is an unthinking nation, and its people are in mortal danger.

America's deepest problems come from blindness to the goodness and power of God. These are the products of unthankfulness.

What should we be thankful for? For the fulfilling of the needs of life, for food to feed our families, and for the means to help the hungry.

Do you give thanks before eating? Jesus did. Again and again, we read that He lifted His eyes toward heaven and offered thanks before beginning the simplest meal. We should be thankful every day, not simply now and then. We should be thankful for clothing to keep our families warm and houses to give them shelter, for life's privileges and freedoms. We should be thankful for God Himself. But are we?

Some months ago, a college student was deeply troubled. He was doing well in school. He had no special money problems. But he was depressed and even fearful. Life had no meaning and no purpose.

Then something happened. While reading a book on prophecy, the things he had learned about God, the Bible, and Jesus Christ began to fit together. A new light came into his life as he realized that the Gospel is all true. He began to understand God's love in that Christ died for him to give him a place in His eternal plan. That very night he confessed Christ as his Saviour and began a new and vital relationship, a new life!

This young man came alive when he saw that God was in the picture. It happens every day when people come to Jesus Christ. "The people which sat in darkness saw great light," we read in Matthew's gospel, "and to them which sat in the region and shadow of death light is sprung up" (Matt 4:16).

Has this light come into your life? If it has, be thankful every day you live.

We should be thankful for many other reasons, but let me mention just one more.

121

3. Because all the circumstances of life are in God's hands

First Thessalonians 5:18 commands, "In every thing give thanks." This means in every circumstance, in every situation. Only the child of God can really do this. But if you belong to Christ, this is your privilege. God will make all things work together for good. Nothing He does is unplanned or capricious.

Times of tears will come, but as we trust and thank Him in "all things," He will fill our lives to overflowing. We need to be thankful in all things, to recognize the hand of God in sorrow as well as joy.

In contrast, how careful we should be about unthankfulness. To become unthankful is to become nearsighted, even blind. The unthankful person no longer sees God's goodness to him. In time, he may forget that he needs God or that God even exists. And when men give up God, God will, in time, give up with men.

What happens in this tragic situation? The description of Romans 1:21 is terribly graphic. "Because that, when they knew God, they glorified him not as God, *neither were thankful;* but became vain [empty, or foolish] in their imaginations, and their foolish heart was darkened" (italics added).

Verse 26 continues, "For this cause God gave them up unto vile affections." And in verse 28, we find this added statement: "And even as they did not like to retain God in their knowledge, God gave them over to a reprobate mind"—a mind incapable of good.

My friend, the price of unthankfulness is high. You cannot ignore God's rights, God's sovereignty, God's loving-kindness, without losing touch with the One on whom your very life depends.

Can a nation slip off into darkness because it is unthankful? It can! It can! America's deepest troubles can be traced to unthankfulness and the folly of forgetting God.

122

Perhaps we have drifted farther than we know in the past three hundred and fifty years. In all their poverty, the Pilgrims were rich because they saw God clearly. Their faith was in Him. They looked to Him for help and sustenance, and He helped them.

Not so with America today. We have lost much of our basic trust in God. No longer do we clearly see His wisdom, power, and love. We have put our trust in men and they are failing. We have laid aside the Bible, not only in our schools, but in our homes and in our public life as well. Small wonder we have lost our concept of sin, our condemnation of wrongdoing. Bloodshed and violence fill our land. Again and again, we have affirmed the rights of men at the cost of God's rights. We have sold our godly birthright for humanism's pottage.

If God were to speak to America through a prophet, He could say to us as He did of Israel through Jeremiah, "For my people have committed two evils; they have forsaken me the fountain of living waters, and hewed them out cisterns, broken cisterns, that can hold no water" (Jer 2:13).

Where have we missed the way? We have made the fatal error of thinking we can be wise and good without God's help, that we can be great and happy and still reject salvation on God's terms. We must turn back. There is no better place to begin than to look up in gratitude this Thanksgiving and renew our faith in God.

CONCLUSION

Apart from the national issue, there is a personal question here. How is it with you this Thanksgiving season? Are you thankful? Can you look up and thank God every day, even sometimes through tears?

It's not a question of how much we have. Some of the most joyous and thankful people that I know live in very modest surroundings. They eat simply. They seldom take a trip. Some of them know infirmity. Why are they thankful? Because they live in the sunshine of God's love.

Are you one of God's thankful people? If not, you should be. God loves you. He made you and redeemed you. He wants to make your eternal soul "shine as the brightness of the firmament; and . . . as the stars for ever and ever" (Dan 12:3).

Jesus Christ came to separate us from our sins. He died on the cross so that you and I might know true forgiveness. Have you let Jesus Christ do what He came to do? In thankfulness receive God's "unspeakable gift."

FIFTEEN

THE FIRST CHRISTMAS

INTRODUCTION

Christmas is probably the happiest day of the year!

Around the world for millions of young and old alike, this special day will again bring joy and happiness. Christmas Day is a special day. There is gladness and singing; there are decorations and presents. And, of course, there will be that special meal and a visit from all the relatives. These are some of the things that make Christmas a day to remember.

For the Christian, Christmas means a lot more than gifts and decorations. Christmas is a great day of joy, victory, and deliverance for the true believer. Dr. Robert Lee has said, "Christmas is the joyous celebration of eternity's intersection with time: 'When the fulness of the time was come, God sent forth his Son, made of a woman' (Gal 4:4)."[1]

Yes, the first Christmas celebration ever held was because of the birth of Jesus Christ. Any other reason for celebrating Christmas is false, foolish, and even sacrilegious!

Let's go back in our minds to the night when Jesus was born. On that first Christmas, there were all the elements of a magnificent worship service. What do we know about the first Christmas service? Look with me for a few moments at what the gospel writer, Luke, has to say about the most important night in history.

1. THE AUDIENCE

First, we read about the audience on that first Christmas. Who were they? "There were in the same country *shepherds* abiding in the field, keeping watch over their flock by night" (Luke

1. Walter B. Knight, *Knight's Illustrations for Today* (Chicago: Moody, 1970), p. 46.

2:8, italics added). That's remarkable! The greatest news story of all ages came to common, hardworking shepherds!

The life of a shepherd was not an easy one. Their work demanded long hours. It meant cold nights and separation from their families. They earned their living watching sheep in a rough, rugged land, a land inhabited by wild animals. Authorities tell us that these shepherds probably did not even own the sheep they tended. Rather, they were lowly, ill-clad hired hands of the religious leaders who raised animals for sacrifice in the Temple.

The greatest news story of history came not to the pious Levites, or to the scholarly religious leaders, or to the Roman governor, or even to King Herod. No, it came to the shepherds of the hills.

But why did God announce such great news to these humble laborers? Were they the only people awake at that important hour? I think He announced it to them because God delights to reveal His Good News to the lowly. The great commoner Abraham Lincoln once said, "God must love the plain people because He made so many of them."

The apostle Paul wrote, "For ye see your calling, brethren, how that not many wise men after the flesh, not many mighty, not many noble, are called: but God hath chosen the foolish things of the world to confound the wise; and God hath chosen the weak things of the world to confound the things which are mighty; and base things which are not, to bring to nought things that are: that no flesh should glory in his presence" (1 Cor 1:26-29).

That is often the way God works. Why? That no flesh should glory. That no mortal man might boast. Can you imagine how a public relations firm might have handled this event? It certainly would have been the opposite of God's approach.

When God chose a leader for Israel, He found Moses on the back side of the desert. When He chose a king, it was the youngest son of the smallest tribe—David. When Jesus chose His

128

twelve disciples, He chose fishermen and tax collectors. Often, He chose the humble and the lowly.

Could it be that the shepherds of the first Christmas were chosen to receive the angel's message because they were humble men of simple origin? Yes, I believe so. There is something rugged and real about the common man. There is an honesty which can respond to God's revelation in a genuine way.

But more, to choose the shepherds on that first Christmas was also fitting because Jesus often pictured Himself as the Good Shepherd. Jesus says, in John's gospel, "I am the good shepherd, and know my sheep, and am known of mine" (John 10: 14). Peter wrote, "When the chief Shepherd shall appear, ye shall receive a crown of glory that fadeth not away" (1 Pet 5: 4). In Luke 15, it was the shepherd who went to seek and save the lost.

Incredible as it may seem, the first audience at that first Christmas service was made up of rough, rugged, lowly shepherds.

2. THE PREACHER

Second, notice the preacher at that first Christmas service: the angel of the Lord. In Luke's gospel we read, "And, lo, the angel of the Lord came upon them, and the glory of the Lord shone round about them: and they were sore afraid" (Luke 2:9).

What a contrasting sight that must have been—the lowly shepherds confronted by the angel of the Lord. And when the angel came upon them, the shepherds sensed that they were in the presence of God, for that is what "the glory of the Lord" shining around them signified. You see, to any Jew, the presence of God was thought of as a great light known as the Shekinah glory. This symbolic light began back in the days of the tabernacle in the wilderness. Man could not see God Himself, but he could see the light of God's presence.

At that first Christmas service, the angel of the Lord appeared to the shepherds, and they were suddenly surrounded by the glory of the Lord. Oh, that we today might be aware of God's

129

glory. God *has* revealed Himself. He has intervened in time and space.

The shepherds saw the revelation of God's presence and they were terrified. They were overcome with fear because their sinfulness was so obvious in the pure light of God's glory.

Of course they were terrified. The holy presence of God always strikes conviction in sinful man. Job experienced that fear when he said, "I have heard of thee by the hearing of the ear: but now mine eye seeth thee. Wherefore I abhor myself, and repent in dust and ashes" (Job 42:5-6). Isaiah, too, when he saw the glory of God filling the Temple, could only say, "Woe is me! for I am undone" (Isa 6:5).

The holiness of God and the sinfulness of man present such a contrast that man must shrink away in awe. The shepherds were afraid as "the glory of the Lord shone round about them."

3. THE MESSAGE

Third, notice the message that the angel of the Lord delivered at that first Christmas service. Luke relates that "the angel said unto them, Fear not: for, behold, I bring you good tidings of great joy, which shall be to all people. For unto you is born this day in the city of David a Saviour, which is Christ the Lord" (Luke 2:10-11).

At the very moment of the shepherds' fear came the joyous message of Christmas: "Fear not. . . . For unto you is born . . . a Saviour, which is Christ the Lord." The Gospel of Jesus Christ is the cure for fear.

A certain degree of fear is a normal reaction in life. In fact, it often protects us from wrong. Abnormal fear, on the other hand, tangles the mind. It destroys peace and drains our energies. More people commit suicide than die from the five most communicable diseases. Why? Because of abnormal fear! One-half of the hospital beds in the United States are occupied by mental patients who suffer from abnormal fears. A well-known doctor told me recently that 60 percent of his patients could cure *themselves* if they could get rid of fear.

What is the medicine for fear? It is the message of Christmas, that a Saviour is born. A Saviour who can forgive you of sin. A Saviour who can give you new life. A Saviour who can strengthen you, guide you, and bring order and purpose into your life.

Paul wrote, "For God hath not given us the spirit of fear; but of power, and of love, and of a sound mind" (2 Tim 1:7). The angel's message at that first Christmas service was, "Fear not!" And in this day of fear—fear of death, fear of war, fear of one another—that message is more relevant than it has ever been before.

But after stressing the negative, "Fear not," the angel accented the positive words of the Christmas message: "I bring you good tidings of great joy." That first Christmas message was one of great joy. Why? Because Jesus came to provide a way out of our dilemma. Jesus Christ came to provide forgiveness and life everlasting.

My friend, Christianity overflows with joy. God's people are to be the happiest people you will find. Whatever your capacity is today, God can fill you with Himself. David wrote, "Be glad . . . rejoice . . . and shout for joy, all ye that are upright in heart" (Psalm 32:11). To the defeated and discouraged, Jesus spoke words of joy: "In the world ye shall have tribulation: but be of good cheer; I have overcome the world" (John 16:33).

Do you know victory today? Have you experienced the joy of that first Christmas message? The New Testament begins with the angels singing a message of comfort and closes with God's children singing joyously around God's throne. True Christianity abounds with joy! Do you know this contagious, irrepressible, holy joy?

4. THE RESPONSE

I believe there is an aspect of the Christmas story which is

131

neglected. It has to do with the fact that those common shepherds had to act upon what they heard on that night long ago. There was a response to that first Christmas service. It was a great thing to hear the news concerning the birth of the Saviour, but mere knowledge was not enough. Could those shepherds have gone back to their "business as usual" after hearing the announcement of the angel? Of course not! They could never, never be the same.

They made an immediate decision. The Bible tells us that they "came with haste" (Luke 2:16). They didn't ask questions. They were fully persuaded, and they acted upon the message which had been given to them. It meant, of course, that they had to leave the sheep, but obviously they knew that what they were about to do was far more important than their flocks.

Perhaps you today have heard this Christmas message; you have realized your need; but you have never made a decision to follow Jesus Christ. You may be reluctant to act on the Good News of Jesus Christ because of your job. Perhaps family ties are standing in the way. Maybe you consider the cost of following Christ too great. My friend, leave the sheep behind and come with haste to Christ today.

The Bible tells us that the shepherds hurried to the village of Bethlehem "and found Mary, and Joseph, and the babe lying in a manger" (Luke 2:16). God rewarded them with the realization of their faith, for they saw their Messiah, the One who had come to be their Saviour.

We are also told that the shepherds immediately shared their discovery. The Good News was too good to keep. My friend, it is wrong to keep silent when we have met the Saviour. The shepherds "made known abroad the saying which was told them concerning this child" (Luke 2:17).

Luke continues by saying that the shepherds "returned, glorifying and praising God for all the things that they had heard and seen" (Luke 2:20). They went back to their common toil, but never to be the same. They had been transformed.

132

Yes, when you receive Jesus Christ as your Lord and Saviour, praising God becomes the very emphasis of your life. Jesus Christ makes the most common of tasks exciting. Glory and praise to God become as natural as breathing.

CONCLUSION

Have you experienced this kind of life? You can! By acknowledging that the Christ of Christmas came to be *your* Saviour from sin, and by committing your life to Him, you may know eternal life. Why not receive Him right now and make this Christmas the most dynamic and happiest you have ever experienced.

SIXTEEN

THE WISDOM
OF THE WISE MEN

No doubt from your earliest recollections of the Christmas story, you recall hearing of the wise men who came to visit the newborn Christ Child. Each of us has sung many times the carols that tell their story. We can even visualize these imposing potentates riding their camels through the desert sands, dressed in their colorful kingly robes.

But who were they? And what do we really know about them?

Really, we do not know a great deal about these wise men. We are not sure who they were. We only have a general idea of where they came from. We can only surmise as to how they knew to follow the star in the heavens. In fact, we don't even know how many there were.

They seem to come out of nowhere, pay their respects to the Christ Child, and then disappear. Matthew's gospel gives us the record of their journey. "Now when Jesus was born in Bethlehem of Judaea in the days of Herod the king, behold, there came wise men from the east to Jerusalem, saying, Where is he that is born King of the Jews? for we have seen his star in the east, and are come to worship him" (Matt 2:1-2).

Who were these wise men? Probably, they were religious philosophers from Persia who, in their contact with the Jews scattered throughout the East, had become familiar with the Jewish Law and prophecies. For many years the report that a world conqueror would be born in Judea had been circulated throughout the Eastern nations. Many Gentiles of that day prayed for a "deliverer" to come, for they clearly realized that their heathen gods could not save them.

Two thousand years before, God had made a promise to Abraham, the father of the Hebrew people, which said, "In thee shall all families of the earth be blessed" (Gen 12:3). The prophet Isaiah, too, had elaborated on the blessing promised to Abraham when he wrote, "And the Gentiles shall come to thy light, and kings to the brightness of thy rising" (Isa 60:3).

Although these wise men were Gentiles, they obviously had a great interest in the fulfillment of God's promise to Abraham. They were intelligent and searching men, and they believed the Word of God as they had heard it.

But even though we are not given a great amount of information about these men, we can determine why they were called "wise men" simply by understanding what they did.

1. THEY FOLLOWED GOD'S DIVINE LEADING

The wisdom of the wise men centered first in the fact that they followed God's divine leading.

How they learned of the prophecy concerning the Messiah, we do not know. What we do know is that they believed that God would lead them to the Christ Child. It was natural that these wise men should be familiar with the heavenly bodies. Undoubtedly they had searched the skies for many days seeking a sign of the birth of the King. To their receptive minds, the guiding star was the finger of God moving across the heavens, and they followed that star.

Are you sensitive to God's leading? This truth has not changed from that day to this. The truly wise man is the one who follows the leading of God. These learned men from the East were not given a road map to follow; they were simply given a star. They followed the light they had, and God honored them for it.

Someone has said that, "the way to see far ahead in the will of God is to go ahead just as far as you can see." That is so true! God does not always outline our entire journey, but He does lead our every step.

The writer of Proverbs tells us that if we acknowledge God in all our ways, He will direct our path (Prov 3:6). God gave the children of Israel a cloud by day and a pillar of fire by night to follow. He gave the wise men a star to lead them. It is true that He does not deal with most of us that dramatically, but He has promised to go before us. If we are willing to take *one* step toward the Lord, He will take *two* steps toward us! Wise men today, as always, are those who follow divine leadership.

2. THEY RESPONDED IN FAITH

Second, the wise men were wise because they responded in faith.

I am sure that their friends must have thought these wise men were out of their minds. "Where are you going?" they were asked. "Well, we don't really know," the wise men had to answer. "We don't know who this new King is or where to find Him. We don't have any idea how long our journey will take or how much it will cost."

And I imagine the wise men were asked, "Well, why do you want to take this foolish and dangerous trip? Why are you going to all this trouble?" "Why?" the wise men must have replied. "Because we have heard a story from Scripture; we have seen the star in the sky; and we have felt a stirring in our souls."

Like Abraham of old, the wise men went out, not knowing whither they went. And wise men of every generation have done the same. William Carey, an English shoemaker, read our Lord's Great Commission. He realized the responsibility of taking the Gospel to every creature. In the face of severe opposition and ridicule, he traveled to that far-off land of India and labored seven years before he saw even one soul won to Christ. He worked relentlessly and translated the Bible into several languages. And he became known as the "father of modern missions."

David Livingstone demonstrated the same venture of faith as he pioneered with the Gospel message throughout the continent

137

of Africa. C. T. Studd, an all-star cricketer from Cambridge, England, forsook fame and fortune and poured out his life in missionary work. He, too, traveled by faith. When Jim Elliot and four other men were murdered by the Auca Indians, some were critical of their attempts to penetrate that savage people with the Gospel. "What a waste," some people cry. "How foolish to throw your life away for nothing." But when the book of God is finally opened, all of these will be listed as wise men, men who ventured forth in faith.

I wonder if you and I can say we have used the opportunities we have had. Have we demonstrated genuine faith? Have we been "wise men" or "foolish men"?

3. THEY WERE WISER THAN THE WORLDLY WISE

Third, the wisdom of the wise men was unique.

God's wise men are always wiser than worldly wise men.

After losing the star on their westward trip, the wise men decided to seek further information concerning the new King. Surely in Jerusalem they would be told where He could be found. They came saying, "Where is he that is born King of the Jews? for we have seen his star in the east, and are come to worship him" (Matt 2:2).

I imagine the wise men expected to find all of Jerusalem worshiping at the feet of this new King. But such was not the case. In fact, Matthew records, "When Herod . . . heard these things, he was troubled, and all Jerusalem with him" (Matt 2:3).

No one in the religious center seemed to be aware of the Messiah's birth. When the frightened Herod demanded of the chief priest and scribes where this Christ should be born, they had to go to the Scriptures. It was from the Old Testament prophecies that the religious leaders were able to determine that Christ would indeed be born "in Bethlehem of Judaea" (Matt 2:5).

But in spite of the fact that these learned men came up with the correct answer, in spite of their knowledge, these religious leaders never did find Jesus. The scribes and priests represented

138

the wisdom of this world. They *knew* but they did nothing! The men from the East were God's true wise men. They believed His word and *did* something. They acted upon it. Their theology was scant, but their obedience was complete. And the Bible tells us that the same "star, which they saw in the east, went before them, till it came and stood over where the young child was" (Matt 2:9). God led them to the Christ Child. Heavenly wisdom is always far superior to earthly wisdom.

4. THEY WORSHIPED THE CHRIST CHILD

Fourth, the wisdom of the wise men was demonstrated in the fact that they worshiped the Christ Child.

In Matthew 2:10-11 we read, "When they saw the star, they rejoiced with exceeding great joy. And when they were come into the house, they saw the young child with Mary his mother, and fell down, and worshiped him."

Charles Lamb was once discussing the greatest literary characters of all time when the names of both William Shakespeare and Jesus Christ were mentioned. "The major difference between these two," said Charles Lamb, "is that if Shakespeare came into this room we would all stand in honor and respect. But if Jesus Christ were here, we would all humbly bow and worship Him."

The wise men had come a long way by faith. But more than that, they entered the house, fell on their knees, and worshiped the Christ Child.

Perhaps you, today, are just like the wise men, seeking to know the Lord. You may have come to the very brink of giving your life to Christ, but you have stopped short of that goal. You have acknowledged your need of a Saviour, but you have failed to enter into His open arms of love.

The Bible tells us that the wise men entered into the house, saw the child, and worshiped Him. They had journeyed by faith, and now they entered in and worshiped by faith.

So many in our world today say, "Show me, and *then* I'll be-

139

lieve." But God's way turns it around. He invites us to *believe*, and then we will see. Believing means seeing. The wise men believed God, and they were rewarded with sight.

But there is more!

The wise men not only worshiped the Christ Child, they presented gifts unto Him. The gold, frankincense, and myrrh were an indication of their love and adoration. This is the reason they had come. This is why they had journeyed so far. When a person has truly come to know Christ, the outpouring of gifts of love are sure to follow. This is what Christmas is all about. God's gift to us is His Son, Jesus Christ. And in return, God desires a gift of you: your heart, your life. The great hymn writer Isaac Watts has said:

> Were the whole realm of nature mine,
> That were a present far too small;
> Love so amazing, so divine,
> Demands my soul, my life, my all.

CONCLUSION

I wonder how far you have come on this journey of faith. Are you still searching and asking, "Where is He?" Or have you received the Saviour? Have you given your life to Jesus Christ the King?

Won't you today, with the wisdom of the wise men, accept Him as your Saviour and Lord?

SEVENTEEN

THE
COSTLIEST
CHRISTMAS

INTRODUCTION

Many people today are concerned about our growing preoccupation with Christmas giving and getting. Gifts keep getting more and more expensive. Increasingly the Christmas season seems swallowed up by shopping, wrapping and mailing packages, and sending cards.

Christmas sales in recent years have hovered at near-record levels. Retailers traditionally expect to conduct more than 15 percent of their annual business during the month of December. Many companies count on heavy Christmas sales to end the year in the black.

While many families this season will give useful gifts and probably less expensive items, stores like Nieman-Marcus say that shoppers seem more willing than ever to buy expensive gifts. These may range from boat cruises and mink coats to Chinese junks at $11,500 each, an adjustable mirror which will make the owner look as thin or rounded as he likes, or even a luxurious bathroom with gold-plated basin and fixtures.

Who will give the world's most expensive Christmas gift this year? What will it be, and how much will it cost? Will it be given by a king or prince or billionaire?

No one knows, of course, but we do know about the world's most costly gift—a gift with you in mind. It was given to the whole human race two thousand years ago. Nearly everyone knows at least a little about this costly gift. It was a child, born in a stable in Bethlehem and laid in a manger. His birth announcement was made from heaven by angels. Word of His coming was beamed by a very special star. Wise men from the East brought Him costly gifts.

No fact in history is so well attested as is the birth, life, and death of Jesus Christ. *Encyclopaedia Britannica* devotes more words to Jesus than to Aristotle, Cicero, Julius Caesar, or the great Napoleon. No life has been so carefully examined, so carefully noted. No life has reached down so many centuries with so great an impact on so many millions of people.

The most costly Christmas of all time brought the gift we need the most: a Saviour, the Holy Son of God. This is the Good News we read in Luke 2:10-11: "Fear not: for, behold, I bring you good tidings of great joy, which shall be to all people. For unto you is born this day in the city of David a Saviour, which is Christ the Lord."

A savior is one who saves. He does for us what we cannot do ourselves.

Joan of Arc was credited with saving France from the total domination of the British. In a similar way, the Duke of Wellington is credited with being the savior of Western Europe, because he turned back Napoleon at Waterloo.

But such great leaders have saved nations only from temporary perils, dangers outside themselves. Jesus saves us permanently from deadly foes within. Can Jesus Christ really save you from the effects of sin? That's an important question, the most important question of all time. Do you need what Jesus can give you? God says yes to both these questions. Around the world, an army of liberated men and women could stand and say, "Jesus has saved me from sins that once spoiled my life. He has made my life new."

Not one who has come to Jesus Christ in sincerity has ever been disappointed or let down. The young person hooked by dope, the "successful" man or woman tangled by pride and selfishness, the person enslaved by lust or bowed down by guilt— all these have found in Jesus Christ the very help they need.

God does not change. Several hundred years before Christ's

144

birth at Bethlehem, God made the promise recorded in Isaiah 1: "Though your sins be as scarlet, they shall be as white as snow; though they be red like crimson, they shall be as wool" (v. 18). God gave the greatest gift of history to keep that greatest promise of history.

In the Christmas story you remember that Joseph, the husband of Mary, was greatly troubled. "Fear not to take unto thee Mary thy wife," God told him in Matthew 1, "for that which is conceived in her is of the Holy Ghost" (v. 20). And then God added, "And she shall bring forth a son, and thou shalt call his name JESUS [the name means Saviour] for he shall save his people from their sins" (v. 21).

The greatest, most costly gift since time began is the Saviour. He bought and paid for the pardon God offers each one of us today. Only Jesus can save His people from their sins.

Why was God's gift so costly? There are three important reasons.

1. THE GREATNESS OF THE NEED

The world and its people's future were at stake. Sin had made havoc of God's creation. It had brought estrangement from its Creator. There were darkness, guilt, and the fear of death.

Seneca, the Roman philosopher, said, "All my life I have been trying to climb out of the pit of my sin, but I cannot and will not unless a hand is let down to lift me." Sin has gripped men's hearts so they cannot change themselves. Apart from Jesus Christ there is no hope, no help. Are you like that today? Unless you have received God's gift, the Bible says you are helpless and hopeless.

2. THE GREATNESS OF THE GIFT

Not only was the need so great, the gift was great! God gave His Son. "This is my beloved Son," He said, "in whom I am well pleased" (Matt 3:17).

The verse which is perhaps the best known in all the Bible is really a Christmas verse: John 3:16, "For God so loved the world, that he gave his only begotten Son." Why? "That whosoever believeth in him should not perish, but have everlasting life."

How much did it cost God the Father to send His Son to the cross for you? The Old Testament gives a beautiful, descriptive picture. Centuries before the birth of Jesus Christ at Bethlehem, God revealed Himself to Abraham, a man of faith. In Abraham's old age, God gave him a son and heir named Isaac. Then came a day when God asked this man of faith to sacrifice his son on Mount Moriah. Though God had other plans, so far as Abraham knew, he was to take the son he loved, travel to Mount Moriah, and offer him there on a lonely mountain altar. As we think of Abraham making that journey with his son, we can picture God's sorrow as Christ moved from Bethlehem to the cross.

But Abraham was spared. At the last minute, as he raised his hand to kill his son, God intervened. But God did not spare *His* Son. He suffered and died to save us from our sins.

3. THE GREATNESS OF THE COST

Read the inspired pictures of the suffering of Christ in Isaiah 53, Psalm 22, and Psalm 69. This great suffering on the cross was only part of the price He gladly paid.

Have you thought of what Jesus left behind, of what it meant for the eternal Son of God to be born in the form of man? He who had done no sin shared sin's effects: a human birth, the trials and sorrows of the life we know, hunger and thirst, fatigue and pain, even the pangs of death.

The Word of God sums it up like this: "Let this mind be in you, which was also in Christ Jesus: who, being in the form of God, thought it not robbery to be equal with God: but made himself of no reputation, and took upon him the form of a servant, and was made in the likeness of men: and being found in fashion as a man, he humbled himself, and became obedient unto death, even the death of the cross" (Phil 2:5-8).

Christ did this willingly for you and me. He says in John 10:17 and 18, "I lay down my life. . . . No man taketh it from me, but I lay it down of myself." Again, in John 15, He says, "Greater love hath no man than this, that a man lay down his life for his friends" (v. 13).

Jesus Christ did not die for sins of His own or because He was the victim of circumstances. He came as God's supreme gift to you and me. What does this mean? It means that you dare not miss this greatest gift. The Bible asks this pointed question: "How shall we escape, if we neglect so great salvation" (Heb 2:3).

But it means *more*. The facts of the most costly Christmas remind us, first, that there are no limits to God's love. "Greater love hath no man than this, that a man lay down his life for his friends" (John 15:13). What more can God do to save you than He has already done?

The most costly Christmas reminds us of God's power. How could God be holy and forgive our sin? How could He take rebellious, sinful people like us and change our hearts and lives? God made all this possible through His great gift!

But the most costly Christmas reminds us of something else which holds a most serious implication. While God's love and power are great, His wrath and judgment upon sin are also real and fearful. If God gave His Son to save us from His judgment of sin, how fearful that judgment must be.

CONCLUSION

The story is told of a family that was experiencing hard times. The father was out of work. The mother had taken a job, but she was earning only a little. Christmas came, and somehow this family managed to have a happy time. There were the usual decorations and even a few small gifts. But everyone felt the financial pressure.

147

The day after Christmas, dad went out once more to look for work, and mother went back to her job. Meanwhile one of the children amused himself by rummaging through the colored paper and ribbon left over from the opened gifts. To his surprise, he found an envelope directed to his father. Later that night, his father opened it and found a generous check, a gift that somehow had been placed with the others, but was almost lost in the wrappings and ribbons of the Christmas season. For that family, the gift turned out to be the beginning of better things.

Could it be that you, too, have overlooked the really important gift of Christmas? Perhaps these moments together have been God's prompting to you to look through the odds and ends of Christmas. God's gift for you is here. Don't miss it. Don't wait to make it yours. Right now, wherever you are, you can receive the costliest gift, Jesus Christ the Saviour.

EIGHTEEN

MAKING ROOM
FOR CHRIST

INTRODUCTION

Where were you born? Most of us would reply by answering, "in a hospital." Some, perhaps, would say, "at home." And occasionally we even hear of an emergency birth in a plane or taxi cab. The circumstances of birth for most of us were very ordinary.

But two thousand years ago, a very uncommon birth took place. It was the birth of Jesus, the Son of God. It was a birth that literally changed the course of the world.

1. NO ROOM AT BETHLEHEM

Luke's gospel tells us that the unusual birth of Jesus Christ took place in an animal stable. God incarnate was born in a stable, "because there was no room . . . in the inn" (Luke 2:7).

But, as unique as the birth of the Christ Child was, it really should have been expected. Centuries before, the Old Testament prophet Isaiah wrote, "The Lord himself shall give you a sign; Behold, a virgin shall conceive, and bear a son, and shall call his name Immanuel" (Isa 7:14).

Seven hundred years before Christ came to earth, the prophet Micah wrote, "But thou, Beth-lehem Ephratah, though thou be little among the thousands of Judah, yet out of thee shall he come forth unto me that is to be ruler in Israel; whose goings forth have been from of old, from everlasting" (Mic 5:2).

Throughout the Old Testament Scriptures, the birth of Jesus Christ is clearly predicted. The place of His birth, His name, His position, all were recorded hundreds of years before Jesus was born in Bethlehem.

From the account in Luke 2, we are given some insight into the secular setting that preceded the Saviour's birth. In that day,

151

Rome was the capital of the world, and Latin was the official language. Caesar Augustus, the supreme ruler of the Roman Empire, sat in his palace on the Tiber River. Luke 2:1 tells us that the emperor, wanting to establish a basis for taxation, decreed that a census was to be taken. This meant that every person in the empire had to be enrolled in his own city.

On the fringe of this great empire, in the little village of Nazareth, soldiers tacked up the order. And Joseph, a builder, an obscure descendant of the great king David, was obliged to go to Bethlehem, the city of David, to register.

Hundreds of years earlier, Micah had prophesied that Bethlehem was to be the place of Christ's birth. The Scriptures proclaimed it to be so. But when Mary and Joseph arrived in the city, there was no room. Of course there was plenty of room for the Roman soldiers who oppressed the people. There was room for the public officials who administered the census. There was room for the wealthy businessmen and merchants. But for Mary and Joseph and the Saviour, soon to be born, there was no room!

Oh, the sadness of those words, "No room in the inn."

In his book entitled *When Iron Gates Yield,* author Geoffrey Bull tells of spending Christmas Eve in a Tibetan inn, enroute to a communist prison camp. As he walked into the stable to feed the horses and mules, he says, "My boots squashed in the manure and straw. The horrible smell of the animals was nauseating, and I thought, 'to think Christ came all the way from heaven to some wretched, eastern stable, and what is more, He came for me.' "

How often we beautify the manger scene. We glorify the hay and straw, the animals, and the shepherds gathered around. And all the while we forget that the Son of God was made to lie in the feeding trough of filthy cattle, that God incarnate was subjected to such abuse and scorn. Why? Because there was no room in the inn or in the hearts of men.

Reginald Heber captured the true perspective of this when he wrote:

152

Cold on his cradle the dew drops are shining,
Low lies his head with the beasts of the stall.

Merson's painting entitled "No Room" depicts a scene of deep shadows, cold stars, a lonely street, and howling dogs, as a hard-hearted innkeeper closes the door and turns Mary away, saying, "No room here."

Yes, in the lowliest place in the world—a barn—the sinless King was born. For the Son of God, the Prince of Peace, there was no room!

2. No room—of course not!

But think of it another way. How could there have been sufficient room for the God-man? How could any earthly inn contain God? Whether an inn, a palace, or a city, no place is large enough to hold the God of the universe.

The apostle John declares, "In the beginning was the Word, and the Word was with God, and the Word was God. The same was in the beginning with God. All things were made by him; and without him was not any thing made that was made" (John 1:1-3). Jesus the God-man—the One who shared the glory of the eternal Father before the world was, He who was present in eternity past, He who created the world and hung the stars in place—how could there be room for Him?

The apostle also declares that it was this Son of God who "was made flesh, and dwelt among us." This is He who was born in Bethlehem's manger, "and we beheld his glory, the glory as of the only begotten of the Father, full of grace and truth" (John 1:14).

Yes, the God-man who said, "Let there be light," who spun the world out of nothing, who scooped out the valleys and piled up the mountains, He became an infant that day. And there was no room.

In one sense we say the whole world is too small to contain Him. But in another sense, we have experienced His habitation within our souls. The songwriter says, "He's big enough to fill the mighty universe, yet small enough to live within the heart."[1]

3. WILL YOU MAKE ROOM?

Do you have room for Jesus?

Consider this phrase in the conventional way. The Bible teaches us that there never was room for Jesus. From His lowly birth in a filthy stable to His burial in a borrowed tomb, there was no room.

As Joseph traveled to Bethlehem with Mary, I am sure he did not envision the problems he would encounter. Surely there would be room for a woman in this condition. No one would turn away an expectant mother soon to give birth to a child.

But as they approached the village that night, they could see that throngs of people had crowded into every nook and cranny. The hustle and bustle of business that first Christmas Eve crowded out the very Saviour of mankind.

How similar to the situation we find in our world today. People get so caught up in the commercialism of Christmas, they do not even see the Christ Child. To many, this day means nothing more than tinsel and gifts and Santa Claus, and that's all. There is no room for Jesus.

How tragic it was that night in Bethlehem! How tragic it is today!

But look a little farther. When the wise men came to Jerusalem looking for the Christ Child, they were questioned by King Herod as to where Jesus could be found. Using the guise of wanting to worship Jesus also, Herod asked the wise men to return when they had found where the young child was. But from that very moment, the wicked king began to secretly plot Jesus' death. For Herod, there was no room for the newborn King.

In Matthew 2:16 we read that when Herod realized the wise men would not return, he "was exceeding wroth, and sent forth,

---

1. Stuart Hamblen, "How Big Is God?" copyright 1958 by Hamblen Music Company, Inc. Used by permission.

154

and slew all the children that were in Bethlehem, and in all the coasts thereof, from two years old and under."

Herod could put out all the lights in Bethlehem, but he could not extinguish that shining star. Herod could still all the infant voices, but he could not silence the angels' singing. He could even kill all the young children, but he could not do away with the Son of God. Herod didn't want God to interfere with his personal plans. He tried to shut Jesus out of his life. He had no room for Jesus. But look on.

When Jesus first journeyed into Galilee to the city of Nazareth, there was again no room for Him. In Luke 4:29, we read that after Christ had preached unto them from the prophets, there arose a great wrath among those that heard Him and they "rose up, and thrust him out of the city, and led him unto the brow of the hill . . . that they might cast him down." His own countrymen rejected Him. They had no room for this carpenter's Son. They would not believe that He was from God.

Again in Luke 8, we find Jesus in Gadara casting out demons. And the account here tells us that when the whole multitude of people saw the power of Jesus, when they saw the demons rebuked, they were terrified and they "besought him to depart from them; for they were taken with great fear" (v. 37). They, too, had no room for Jesus!

Everywhere Jesus went, every time He preached, in every place He performed miracles, He met with opposition. Why? Because the people were unwilling to accept and believe that this was the Son of God. They could not allow this Prophet to interfere with their religious ritual and tradition. Their eyes were blinded. They had no room for Jesus.

What an indictment those words bring!

As Jesus entered into those last hours before the cross, He was so very alone. There was no one, not even the disciples, who had room for Him. As He prayed in the Garden of Gethsemane that night, He sweat, as it were, great drops of blood. He prayed and He suffered all alone!

Did you ever go through a period of time when you felt all alone? Jesus did. The Scriptures tell us that He had no place to lay His head. The rocks were His pillow; the ground, His bed. The wind was His comb, and He was all alone.

We at times can feel very lonely, and I'm sure that Jesus did too. But despite this fact, and despite the fact that we close ourselves off from Him, Jesus is still there waiting for us to make room for Him in our lives.

In Revelation 3:20, He says, "Behold, I stand at the door, and knock: if any man hear my voice, and open the door, I will come in to him, and will sup with him, and he with me."

He calls, but you must answer. He knocks, but you must make room for Him and open the door of your life.

God is all-powerful; He could force open your heart's door. But He does not. Jesus could have been born in a kingly palace. The Saviour could have summoned to earth His angelic armies to capture His tormentors. But He did not. And He never forces us to accept Him. He simply stands and knocks. Patiently He waits for us to respond.

Oh, what a wonderful time this would be for you to make room for Jesus. Someday, my friend, death will knock. Death comes on with rackless footsteps. It is inevitable and unrelenting. And when that day dawns, there will be no more opportunities, no more chances, to open the door of your life.

CONCLUSION

In his famous painting of Christ knocking at the door, artist Holman Hunt has purposely omitted from the door a knob or handle. Why? Because that is on the inside, and you, and you alone, can open the door to Jesus.

Two thousand years ago, on that first Christmas Eve, there was no room for Jesus. Throughout the centuries, men have rejected Him; they have turned their backs on His love. But you, today, have an opportunity to receive Jesus into your life. Why not make room for Jesus right now, and accept Him as your personal Saviour and Lord.